D0234186

S

Lif

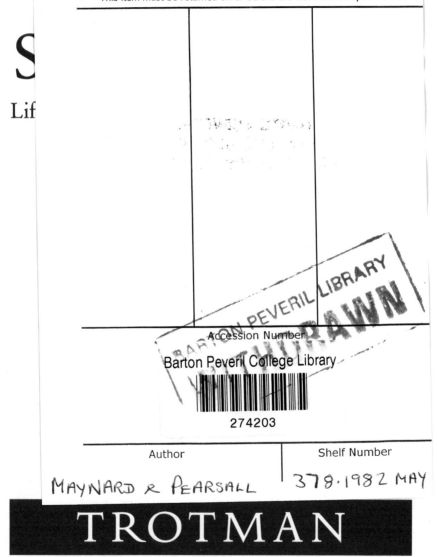

Accession Number	
Barton Peveril College Library	
274203	

Author	Shelf Number
MAYNARD & PEARSALL	378.1982 MAY

TROTMAN

This second edition published in 2001
by Trotman & Company Ltd
2 The Green, Richmond, Surrey TW9 1PL

First edition published 1994

© Trotman and Company Limited 2001

British Library Cataloguing in Publication Data
A catalogue record for this book is available from the
British Library.

ISBN 0 85660 694 4

Typeset by Mac Style, Scarborough, N. Yorkshire
Printed and bound in Great Britain
by Creative Print & Design (Wales) Ltd

CONTENTS

FOREWORD

I am very pleased to be given the opportunity not only to welcome the *Mature Students' Guide*, but also to endorse the importance of lifelong learning.

Since we published the 'Learning Age' Green Paper in 1998, this government has been totally committed to lifelong learning. This is because it is key to social inclusion and to prosperity – for individuals, business and the nation.

Socially, learning helps sustain civilised and cohesive societies. It encourages people to develop as active citizens and play a full part in their local communities. It strengthens families, builds stronger neighbourhoods, helps people remain active and encourages independence for all by opening up new opportunities.

Economically the case for learning becomes stronger by the day. Education and training are the most effective way to increase earning capacity. For example, people with no qualifications earn 20 per cent less than average, 25 per cent less than those with A-levels and 50 per cent less than graduates. People who lack skills and qualifications really do lose out.

And it is not just individuals – employers lose out too. Productivity in the UK falls short of that of many of our leading competitors. Gross domestic product in the UK lags behind the US by almost 40 per cent and behind France and Germany by almost 20 per cent. And if we raised the numeracy skills of all adults to the standard we expect for 11-year-old children we would increase our domestic product by up to £40 billion.

The old traditional manufacturing industries are increasingly being replaced by modern industries – electronics, IT and communications – and as the structure of the economy changes so must the workforce. Unless people have the skills and qualifications they need to adapt to this changing market they will fail to reach their potential and business will be unable to compete and grow.

It is therefore easy to see why lifelong learning is a key manifesto commitment for this government and why our policies seek to maximise participation in and attainment through learning.

Our approach to lifelong learning is based on five broad aims. First, we are rationalising the funding and organisation of learning through the establishment of the Learning and Skills Council (LSC). Launched in April 2001 the LSC will be the most significant and far-reaching reform ever enacted to post-16 learning in this country. For the first time the planning and funding of all post-compulsory education below higher education will be integrated into a single system providing effective co-ordination, promotion and strategic planning for lifelong learning and focusing particularly on skills and employer needs at national, regional and local levels.

Second, we have policies related to financial support for learners. Here we are attempting to break down one of the most common barriers to participation in learning – individuals who cannot afford to pay for their learning. For example we have developed:

- Individual Learning Accounts (ILAs), which offer a package of incentives to help people pay for their learning and development. To date over 600,000 accounts have been opened and we aim to have 1 million accounts opened by 2002.
- The Career Development Loans Scheme, designed to help individuals pay for vocational education and training. In partnership with four major banks, loans of up to £8000 may be applied for to support up to two years of education or training with the government paying the interest on the loan.
- Student loans, to help with students' living costs. All students are entitled to 75 per cent of the maximum loan, with the remaining quarter subject to income assessment. These loans do not have to be repaid until the student has left university or college and is earning over £10,000 a year. They attract interest at the rate of inflation, well below commercial rates. Extra, non-repayable help is targeted at certain students: those with disabilities and dependants; those entering HE from care; and from 2001/02, those entering higher education

from low-income families in inner city areas. Help is also available from universities and colleges for those who get into financial difficulties as students.

- In addition, the free provision of basic skills courses is designed to attract those people who tend to be in the most deprived areas into this type of provision.

Third, we provide information, advice and guidance (IAG) to encourage individuals to take up learning. Whilst we have the Connexions Service for young people aged 13 to 19, we also have information, advice and guidance services for adults, managed by Local Learning Partnerships. These services will help individuals to overcome the barriers to learning, through advice and guidance on issues such as childcare and finance. Local networks of IAG services provide clients with easy access to information and advice services that are free of charge, respond to the needs of the local area and meet nationally endorsed standards of quality. These networks include colleges, job centres, career services, employers, trade unions and voluntary sector bodies. Information, advice and guidance are also available through the learndirect website, which contains a wealth of information on learning and career opportunities. The website supplements the learndirect free learning helpline (0800 100 900), which has already handled over two and a half million calls.

Fourth, our policies support an effective qualifications framework, which aims to raise the standard of learning provision. The qualifications system plays a crucial role in attracting learners and the standards of provision underpin the qualifications framework in that they ensure effective learning towards course goals. High quality standards are needed throughout lifelong learning and it is the job of the inspection regimes to ensure they are met.

Last, we have policies related to work-based training and engaging with employers. Here the aims of policies such as Modern Apprenticeships are to raise attainment by ensuring that we have a quality work-based route that is attractive to learners less inclined to academic learning. We also work with employers through National Training Organisations and Investors in People to ensure that they make a fair and effective contribution to learning.

I wish you success and enjoyment in your studies. Whatever your age, and for whatever reason you have chosen to take up the challenge, it is never too late to start learning.

Malcolm Wicks, MP
Parliamentary Under-Secretary of State for Lifelong Learning

ABOUT THE AUTHORS

Liz Maynard studied for her BA(Hons) and BPhil in social sciences at York University, graduating in 1968. She taught with the Open University, the Workers' Educational Association, and the National Extension College whilst bringing up young children. She completed a teacher training course at 35 and spent most of her career teaching social science at the College of Ripon and York St John. Her experiences of juggling the responsibilities of academic and domestic life have given her a ready sympathy for the special pressures that many mature students have to cope with. She was the College mature student adviser and was involved in setting up the humanities and social science Access course at her local college of further and higher education and continues to liaise with staff and students currently as an external assessor. She is now Disability Coordinator at the College.

Simon Pearsall decided to leave school at 17, much against his parents' wishes. He had a variety of jobs and spells of unemployment until at the age of 33 he took a special entrance exam for mature candidates and became a student at the University College of Ripon and York St John. Despite the difficulties of poorly controlled epilepsy, he flourished at College and was nominated for the Outstanding Adult Learner Award in 1992. In 1991 he was employed on a national CNAA/UDACE research project into the counselling and guidance needs of mature students undertaken at the College. After graduation he was engaged in further research activities into the circumstances and performance of mature students. He is now a civil servant.

'NIACE welcomes the publication of Trotman's *Mature Students' Guide*. It is a practical and accessible guide for anyone planning to return to learning. It makes effective use of the experience of existing learners, to encourage others to take part.'

Alan Tuckett, Director
NIACE, The National Organisation for Adult Learning

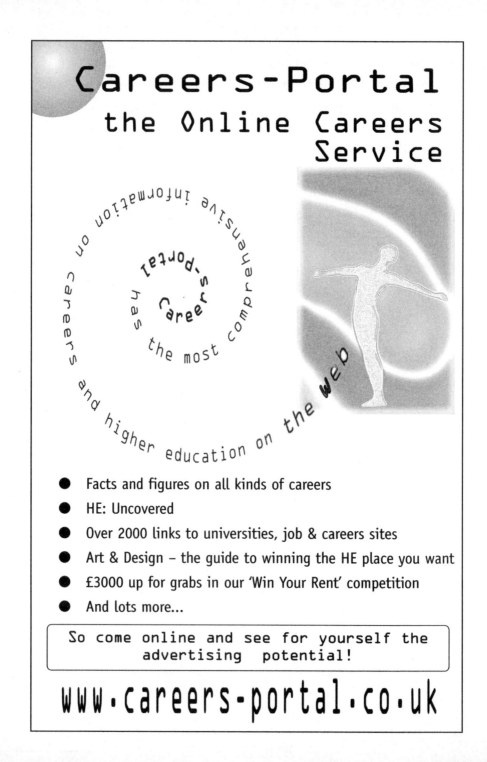

Careers-Portal
the Online Careers Service

Careers-Portal has the most comprehensive information on careers and higher education on the web

- Facts and figures on all kinds of careers
- HE: Uncovered
- Over 2000 links to universities, job & careers sites
- Art & Design – the guide to winning the HE place you want
- £3000 up for grabs in our 'Win Your Rent' competition
- And lots more...

So come online and see for yourself the advertising potential!

www.careers-portal.co.uk

WIN YOUR RENT!
Competition

Competition Entry Form

How To Enter

1   Please <u>underline</u> your answers clearly (a, b or c) for each of the three competition questions below.

2   Complete your name and address details overleaf.

3   Complete the questionnaire overleaf.

1 What is the maximum annual amount UK students attending a university in England or Wales will be asked to pay in tuition fees for the 2001/2002 academic year?

a. £500   b. £750   c. £1,075

2 How much is the average student (not living at home or London based) expected to live on during 2001/2002?

a. £3,815   b. £4,545   c. £5,545

3 What is the threshold annual salary graduates must be earning before they have to start paying back their student loans?

a. £8,000   b. £10,000   c. £12,000

Trotmanpublishing

QUESTIONNAIRE

Name ....

Address ....

....

....

....

Postcode...

Telephone ....

Date of Birth ....

E-mail address ....

Where are you currently studying?
- ☐ School
- ☐ FE College
- ☐ HE College
- ☐ University
- ☐ Other...

What year are you in? ....

What subjects are you taking?

Subjects	Level	Predicted Grades
....	....	....
....	....	....
....	....	....
....	....	....
....	....	....

When will you be sitting your exams? ....

In which year would you like to start university? ....

Do you have internet access?
- ☐ at home   ☐ at school

Which subject areas are you considering studying at Higher Education?
- ☐ Art & Design
- ☐ Business
- ☐ Computer Studies
- ☐ Engineering
- ☐ Medicine/Healthcare
- ☐ Performing Arts
- ☐ Physical Sciences
- ☐ Other...

From which of the following information sources have you sought advice on entering Higher Education?
- ☐ UCAS Big Guide
- ☐ Degree Course Offers
- ☐ UCAS Handbook
- ☐ Student Book
- ☐ University/college literature/prospectuses
- ☐ The Complete Guides
- ☐ Other
- ☐ Internet
  - If so which site? ....

Please photocopy this form and give to your friends

SEND COMPLETED FORMS TO: 'WIN YOUR RENT' COMPETITION, 2 THE GREEN, RICHMOND, SURREY TW9 1PL.

Conditions of entry

1. Entry Forms with three correct answers will be entered into the Prize Draw. The Draw will be made on 1st September each year, and the winner and runners-up will be notified shortly after that date.

2. Prizes: The winner will receive a cheque for £3,000. 100 runners-up will receive copies of the 7th edition of *Students' Money Matters* (RRP £10.99; published May 2001).

3. All competition entrants must be students applying for 2002 entry to university or college, or current students who will still be studying for an undergraduate or postgraduate degree in 2002.

4. Only one entry is allowed per person.

5. No purchase necessary. Separate Entry Forms are available by sending an SAE to the address given above.

INTRODUCTION

'Mature students are well motivated, capable and a pleasure to teach.'

(University lecturer)

Until comparatively recently the possibility of re-entering education for many adults simply never arose. Of late, though, the number of students has increased, of whom a large number have been mature entrants (ie those over the age of 21). In the light of a number of influential government reports, such as the Kennedy Report and the Dearing Report, the government has made a commitment to 'Widening Participation'. It wants to have 50 per cent of the population entering higher education by the age of 30, and through various policy initiatives it is attempting to address the social class imbalance in the student population. The government is recognising that a greater number of today's adults are capable of benefiting from what higher education has to offer, and the advantages to the country of their participation. Within colleges and universities, also, staff are increasingly realising that the educational environment is enriched by an increasingly diverse student population. For instance they often have positive things to say about their experience of mature students:

'It amazes me how these students can cope with the exacting demands of course work, run a home, family, juggle the money, and often as a single parent. I take my hat off to them!'

'They are more realistic, have a wealth of experience, and are a joy to teach, to learn from and to be friends with.'

WHY BECOME AN ADULT LEARNER?

People re-enter education for a variety of reasons and at different times in their lives. Many do so in order to improve or change their

1

employment prospects, or at least as a first step towards a career; others do so for more personal reasons – perhaps because they did not enjoy school, or because their priorities have changed since they were 18. Sometimes the decision is triggered by a period of upheaval in people's lives: divorce, redundancy, bereavement, etc. But more often the desire to return to education occurs because people feel that their existing lives are not personally satisfying – whether it be in employment or at home – and it seems they are going nowhere fast.

'I felt I had to redeem myself after not being very good at marriage.'

(Gill, graduate 2000)

'I went to university as a mature student and also somewhat off the cuff. I had lost a job just before Clearing came round, so I decided for a degree place rather than remain unemployed.'

(Mike Barwise in Tolmie, P. (1998)
How I got my First Class Degree, p.33)

'Cocooned in motherhood, when my children were small I had been happy to dedicate my days to them. As they progressed to school I too felt the need for learning reawaken within me. I had a feeling of emptiness that only intellectual growth would fulfil.'

(Coare, P. and Thomson, A. (1996)
Through the Joy of Learning. Diary of 1,000 Adult Learners)

'Being made redundant after 25 years' service made me realise that personal satisfaction should be moved up the agenda. Ruth and I both had a long-standing ambition to study for a degree at a "conventional" university and we decided it was time to fulfil that ambition.'

(Glyn, who graduated with his wife Ruth in 1998,
A Guide for Mature Students, College of Ripon and York)

Whatever your reasons for considering returning to education, you need to possess certain information if you are to select the best course for your circumstances. It is helpful to have some knowledge of the full range of courses that are available and the institutions in which they are taught. If, for example, you want to do a degree and do not possess A-levels or their equivalents, you need to know how to take advantage of the special admission procedures and preparation courses that exist for older applicants. And the more you know about the selection methods of universities and colleges the better you can prepare your application, and the better chance you have of being accepted.

Equally important, it is essential that you have an accurate picture of life as a student before you make any decisions. Unfortunately, some of the most important considerations are financial. There may be some help available, but it is limited so you would be wise to get yourself as well informed as possible on these aspects of becoming a student. It is also helpful if you have a realistic idea of the work demands of your proposed course, particularly if you are considering full-time study. Although courses involve varying levels of attendance, many students are surprised at the sheer volume of work required.

The purpose of this guide is to provide you with information about returning to education as an older person. It focuses on the steps necessary to enter higher and further education, and is intended to build a positive but realistic picture of what such a step entails.

Chapter 1
WHAT'S ON OFFER?

'Those outside university don't understand the activities that go on here. But their attitudes are often wrong. It's really okay.'

Where you get what qualifications is no longer as clear as it used to be. There are a number of reasons for this. Partly because of the government's commitment to 'Widening Participation' and 'Lifelong Learning', the providers of education have responded by offering a greater number of courses in a greater number of locations. So, while the government is extremely keen to get adults back into education, the plethora of information available from websites, careers services, libraries, colleges and universities, etc has sometimes made it more difficult to find what you actually want to know. At the same time institutions are becoming more fragmented and the divisions between them have become less clear. Nevertheless the distinction between further education and higher education is a relevant one.

Further education (FE) is provided mainly through local colleges; a wide variety of academic, vocational and leisure-oriented courses are taught both to school leavers and older students. Many of the courses available at further education colleges (such as A-levels, BTECs, GNVQs and GCSEs) are entrance qualifications for higher education. There are other special courses for mature students with few formal educational qualifications who want to enter higher education known as Access courses.

'Former crimper Nicola Millington is swapping her scissors to explore the world of Medical Science. The 24-year-old has successfully completed the Access to Higher Education course studying biology, chemistry and maths at Dewsbury College this year. Now she is continuing her studies at Leeds University where she is undertaking a degree in biochemistry and pharmacology this autumn.'

(*Dewsbury Reporter*, quoted in
Access to Higher Education Course Directory 2001)

Higher education (HE) is provided largely through universities and colleges of higher education. Some of the universities are known as 'new' universities – they used to be called 'polytechnics'. These teach degree, diploma, certificate and professional courses in a wide variety of subject areas. The majority of their students will be engaged on three-year degree programmes. The standard entry requirement for these courses is A-levels or their equivalent (eg Scottish Highers and the European Baccalaureate exams), but alternative entrance procedures exist for those who are over 21 when they start their studies.

As we said, distinctions between these institutions are breaking down and it is now possible to do at least some degree work at FE colleges, and universities are offering more sub-degree level work. The new universities used to offer more vocational courses than the old universities, but the differences are becoming much less pronounced. The 'old' universities still enjoy somewhat superior status and receive higher levels of funding than the new universities. The old universities also tend to have fewer mature students than the new universities.

Colleges of higher education

There are a number of institutions that are not universities where is it possible to study for a degree: colleges of higher education. These mostly started life as teacher training colleges, and they continue to undertake a large responsibility for such work today. But, in addition, in more recent years these colleges have diversified into providing all sorts of other courses, mainly at first degree level.

THE HIGHER EDUCATION AWARDS

'I've less of a chip on my shoulder. I now realise that the academic world is not the unreachable thing I thought before.'

The majority of students in higher education are engaged on degree courses, and are known as undergraduates. Most full-time degree courses last for three years, whereupon the successful students graduate and are awarded 'Bachelor's' degrees. These courses have a comparatively high level of contact time with teaching staff, and are also sometimes known as 'first degrees'. The most common degree titles are:

- BA Bachelor of Arts
- BSc Bachelor of Science
- BEng Bachelor of Engineering

Some first degree courses last longer than three years, particularly those related to a specific professional training, such as architecture or medicine. Many other degrees would include a 'year out', working in an occupation related to the degree subject. Examples of this would include computing science and surveying courses. Language degrees would usually involve a year abroad in a country that speaks the chosen language. In contrast, a part of the Widening Participation programme has been the encouragement of Foundation degrees, which are designed to provide qualifications and skills that will be recognised by employers but that last for only two years and can be converted to full first degrees with a further year of study.

Whilst many mature students opt to study for three-year first degrees, others decide to do a **Higher National Diploma** (HND) or **Higher National Certificate** (HNC). A full-time HND course lasts for two years, and tends to be more oriented towards a particular sphere of employment than most degree courses. They are also often accepted as a qualification for entry on to a related degree course, and it is sometimes possible to enter into the second year of the degree programme if you have an HND. One diploma course that is now based in universities is the three-year nursing diploma and this is a course which attracts many older students.

There are also 'higher' or **Master's degrees** (eg MA, MSc, MPhil) and doctorates or PhDs), which can follow on from first degrees, and that place more emphasis on individual research than first degrees. Higher degrees and some postgraduate diplomas normally require the student to have achieved highly on their first degree.

Degree classifications

The classifications for honours degrees are as follows:

First
Upper Second (2:1)
Lower Second (2:2)
Third
Pass
Fail

The Pass category does not usually count as an 'honours' degree; it is also possible to study for an 'Ordinary' (ie non-Honours) degree in some institutions.

STUDENT FACILITIES AND SERVICES

The vast majority of universities and colleges of higher education aim to be relatively self-sufficient communities. These provide their members not only with academic amenities such as libraries, workshops and computer workstations, but also a range of personal support services such as shops, catering facilities, nurseries or crèches, living accommodation, health centres, and sports, pastoral, recreational and religious amenities. These are available to all students, whatever their age, and whether or not they live in university or college accommodation. In general, universities tend to be large, with Leeds University the biggest with 24,000 students on degree programmes and a further 24,000 on short courses; whereas the smallest university, Lampeter, has approximately 1400 students. Of course, the amenities on the university or college campus vary according to the number of students they are serving. FE colleges recruit most of their students locally and therefore do not usually provide residential accommodation.

Many amenities are often provided by or with the assistance of the Students' Unions, which exist to represent students' interests at institutional and national level as well as providing a variety of student-run services on the campus. They will often help organise mature student societies, and may appoint officers to represent the special interests of mature students on their organising committees. All students automatically become members of the Students' Union when they enrol at university or college.

WHAT SUBJECTS CAN YOU STUDY?

The government's Widening Participation programme has encouraged the development of all sorts of courses for all sorts of purposes. There are hundreds of different courses available to you at a variety of levels. Some courses are aimed at developing your skills in the workplace; others at helping your personal development; and still others at pursuing an interest or hobby. Of course you can choose to do more than one course at a time.

> 'Well, here I am, retired and in my seventies, but still attending four classes a week. In this day and age I feel it behoves everyone to know something about computers and their uses. I tried teaching myself at home from books for four months, then I decided to join my information technology, desktop publishing and word processing courses. At least now I can talk to my 12-year old godson.'
>
> (Coare, P. and Thomson, A. (1996)
> *Through the Joy of Learning. Diary of 1,000 Adult Learners*)

Undergraduates usually specialise in a single subject area, or discipline, throughout their time in higher education. Some of these are similar to the subjects studied at school, such as history, English literature and maths, but many other subjects not usually available in schools, such as environmental science, tourism management and women's studies, are taught in higher education.

Virtually all universities and colleges of higher education are organised into subject-based departments, which in turn are sometimes grouped into larger 'schools' or 'faculties'. During their time in higher education students follow a 'programme' of study, which consists of a fixed number of separate courses (or 'modules' in many institutions). Students are usually able to exercise a significant level of choice in determining the content of their individual programme, but some courses may be compulsory, particularly at the outset of the programme. For example, English literature students may well be required to study at least one Shakespeare course or module, but will have a choice over whether they study, say, 20th-century poetry or black American writers.

Most students base all their courses in the programme within a single discipline. However some students, instead of following one main subject, study for a joint honours or a combined honours degree and split their time between two or more subject areas. For example a student taking both social sciences and linguistics may focus primarily on social sciences as a 'major' subject and so spend less time on linguistics, the 'minor' subject. Alternatively, in joint honours degrees, students will spend an equal amount of time studying both subjects.

HOW DO STUDENTS LEARN?

'I wasn't sure what was expected, what level of work. But there have been no problems.'

One of the features of higher education that mature students appreciate is the fact that the way they are taught is very different from the way they were taught in school. The method of teaching and learning will to some extent depend on the nature of the discipline, but the most common methods are:

- *Lectures* – in which a tutor talks at length to a large group (anything from 15 to 150), usually for around an hour. Students are expected to listen and make notes, and not to participate actively until a time for questions at the close.
- *Seminars* – in which relatively small groups of students discuss a topic under the supervision of a tutor. Often this is preceded by a presentation by one or more members of the group.
- *Tutorials* – Students are allocated a tutor with whom they can discuss their work individually or in small groups. They may also be allocated a personal tutor or supervisor who can advise on any issue that may impinge on the student's academic work. The student often remains with the same personal tutor for the duration of the degree programme.
- *Practical, or 'hands-on' work* – In some disciplines, such as teaching, art and science subjects, direct experience has always been an essential ingredient of the course. In recent years this approach has been adopted increasingly in other disciplines. For instance, social sciences students may find themselves working on assignments in the

9

community or developing questionnaires to distribute to students or staff around the campus.

■ *Small group work* – Something that virtually all students very quickly find is that one of the most valuable and accessible learning resources at their disposal is other students. This kind of cooperation occurs on an informal basis, of course, but it is increasingly utilised also to facilitate practical or theoretical problem-solving exercises. For example, a social sciences lecturer may frequently divide classes into a number of small groups to discuss certain questions, such as 'Why do people get married?' Once the students have adequate time to explore the issues involved, they then report their conclusions to the class as a whole. Or similar groups may work on assessed project work such as an assignment in the community or on a practical experiment.

'Often mature students like myself were more confident and focused than the younger ones. We would encourage them to speak more openly in seminars, while they gave us new insights we may not have considered.'

(L. Thompson, *Woman and Home*, March 2001, p. 149)

The way to a good degree for most students, however, is still by spending large amounts of time reading, absorbing what they have read, reflecting on it and writing about it. One of the basic skills that students have to develop is note-taking, not only for lectures, tutorials, etc, but also for their reading and for their written work. Computer technology and the Internet have affected studying, and students may be expected to have basic computing skills and to be able to conduct research via the Internet. Some courses may involve the use of computer packages.

In the past it was assumed that all undergraduates came into higher education already equipped with the skills necessary for study such as essay writing, note-taking and using libraries. More recently, though, institutions have recognised the need to provide 'study skills' courses, and these will probably include computer skills.

HOW ARE STUDENTS ASSESSED?

'I had a sense of insecurity until the first academic feedback.'

'I started college feeling very nervous. The entrance hall was full of young school leavers. All that was in my mind, fear, was I going to make a fool of myself ...'

(Margaret Whiting in Coare, P. and Thomson, A. (1996)
Through the Joy of Learning. Diary of 1,000 Adult Learners, p. 144)

Many people who did not do well at school are put off re-entering education because of their fear of exams. Whilst exams do still play the most important part in the assessment process in many courses, the emphasis placed on them is lessening gradually. There are two reassuring points to note: first, that many institutions recognise the particular difficulty that exams pose for some students, especially those who have been out of education for a significant time, and provide practical and moral support for those students who require it. (Many younger students are only too grateful to receive this help as well!)

Second, that continuous assessment is playing a more significant part in measuring each student's progress and attainment. This means that work produced during a particular course is graded and used instead of, or in conjunction with, exams. As well as allowing students to work in the way that suits them best, continuous assessment also provides students with valuable feedback on how they are doing. So if they do well in one piece of work they can feel confident that they are approaching the subject in an appropriate manner; if they don't do so well they can take immediate action to remedy their faults. Such course work is usually in the form of written assignments, but may also take the form of short projects or practical work.

- *Essays and course work* – Students are expected to produce written work on a regular basis for assessment.
- *Presentations* – Many modules now include either individual or group verbal presentations of material. This may also be accompanied by written work.
- *Dissertations* – A feature of course work that frequently appeals to older students is what is sometimes known as a 'dissertation'. A dissertation may stand as a course in its own right. Here students are

encouraged to undertake a fairly lengthy piece of work on a subject of their choosing. Under the supervision of a tutor students research their topic in greater depth than would be the case if it was part of a course, and report on their findings. Again, students are usually given advice on how to equip themselves with the kinds of library and research skills necessary for such a project.

WHO ARE THE OTHER STUDENTS?

'Somehow I managed to fit a social life in with my degree. My friends are varied in age from 19 to 50; some undergraduates, some postgraduates and some workers; both men and women. I probably do less work because of my friends, but I probably enjoy the work I do more.'

(Arksey, H., Marchant, I. and Simmill, C. (1994)
Juggling for a Degree, p.32)

'As a mature student I did at times feel isolated – sometimes taken for granted, but then maybe I should have tried harder to join in conversations about the latest mobile phone designs or Internet chat lines. Maybe I'm jaundiced, but that's what seemed to dominate the conversation of the teenage students who, on my course, were very much in the majority.'

(*The Mature Students' Guide to Higher Education 2001*, p.16)

The popular image of students tends to be a rather privileged group of young people who are not really part of the 'real world'. They are seen as rather work-shy individuals who stay up late, are constantly pleading poverty and have no real responsibilities.

On the other hand the image of students in university and college prospectuses (the handbooks produced annually by each institution as guides for prospective students) often presents an idyllic picture of attractive and wholesome young people earnestly studying or debating amidst scenes of ivy-clad quadrangles, bicycles and medieval streets. Alternatively, students are pictured engaged in worthy pursuits such as community work, mountain climbing, computer programming or dramatic productions, activities that are almost always featured against ultra-modern backdrops or some local beauty spot.

Although the individuals featured in the photographs are no longer exclusively white or male by any means there is one category of students that these pictures rarely represent – mature students. So, while such images contain a fair mix of fact and fiction, what they all fail to convey is a truly realistic idea of students, young and old, and the lives they lead. In particular, they largely ignore the rapid growth in the number of mature students over the past decade. In many institutions mature students account for at least a quarter of all students, and in some places as many as a half. Such students may have left school at 16 or earlier rather than at 18, are any age up to 70, and may have rather more experience of nappies than Nietzsche! What little time mature students have to spare is more likely to be spent working at a part-time job than engaging in the admirable activities portrayed in the prospectuses, though they may often envy the freedom of the younger students to be able to do so. All mature students, of course, are able to take full advantage of the leisure and cultural activites that are part of university (or college) life.

> 'During my three years I took up an activity I used to enjoy at school – trampolining. It was really enjoyable, but after a break of 24 years it wasn't easy.'
>
> (Julie, graduate 2000, *A Guide for Mature Students*, College of Ripon and York)

There exist, then, a number of beliefs and generalisations about who students are, where they come from, and what they do once they are in university or college. Some of these beliefs are simply false, some are out of date, and all of them can inhibit the person who is unfamiliar with higher education from making further enquiries about it.

Education is changing rapidly, becoming more welcoming to a wider range of students than ever before. The number of older students, many of them working class or coming from families that have had no tradition of academic success, is steadily increasing. Universities and colleges are also now more aware of the needs of people with disabilities, and ready and willing to accommodate them.

Chapter 2
IS RETURNING TO EDUCATION REALLY FOR YOU?

'Since going to college I've become more self-confident and I feel a greater sense of worth. It's really broadened my outlook on life.'

The decision to re-enter education is ultimately an act of faith in yourself and your abilities. As such, it is likely to be one of the more significant decisions that you have to make. To do any course is likely to be a major undertaking in itself. If you are thinking of a degree course it will probably require at least three years, during which time it will make constant demands on you. It is important, therefore, that you are sure that you can sustain an interest in the course for which you apply. In addition, your studies will almost inevitably have an impact on other areas of your life. Many mature students who 'drop out' do so not because they lack ability but because other factors – money problems, family, etc – clash with their studies.

'You have to recognise that it is a commitment, it will butt into the social life sometimes, it will get frustrating, there will be tantrums and tears at times, but the end goal is worth it.'

(Sarah Anderton in Tolmie, P. (1998)
How I got my First Class Degree, p.7)

Others, on the contrary, find that higher education enhances their relationships, for example with their own children who are going through school and/or college themselves.

'Obviously education is a high priority in our household and I hope that my own study is an example to my children.'

(Coare, P. and Thomson, A. (1996)
Through the Joy of Learning. Diary of 1,000 Adult Learners, p.23)

'It does children good. They love books and anything to do with learning.'

(Dawn, graduate 1999)

In order that your faith in yourself is justified, it is important for you to be as aware as possible of what you are taking on and to assess whether going back to education is a realistic option for you. You need to ask yourself some perhaps difficult questions about yourself, your circumstances, and those close to you.

WHY DO YOU WANT TO BE A STUDENT?

'Most research on motivation in continuing education suggests that there are three main, overlapping motives for engaging in learning – vocational, academic and personal interest and development.'
(McNair (1996), quoted in Benn, R., Ellott, J. and Whaley, P. *Educating Rita and her Sisters*, p.24)

- Do you want to follow an interest in a particular subject in depth over such a long period of time?
- Do you want to prove to yourself (and possibly others) that you can be successful at this level?
- Do you want to obtain qualifications to enter a specific career, or perhaps progress in your existing work?
- Do you need a stimulus in your life, perhaps because you have spent years at home looking after a family, or are unemployed?
- Are you looking for a new direction because you have reached a crossroads in your life, such as divorce, bereavement or moving house?
- Other reasons?

Mature students re-enter education for a whole variety of reasons, the most common of which are listed above. One or more of these may reflect your own reasons. If you are not entirely clear as to why you want to go back, now is the time to analyse your reasons for wanting to do so. Identifying your own motivation in wanting to enter higher education will help you in two ways: it will enable you to assess whether you are likely to be able to maintain the necessary level of interest in your chosen course, and it will be of immense value when you actually come to the application and interview stages.

WHAT DO YOU HAVE TO OFFER?

'I came to university with mixed feelings, the most dominant being excitement and fear. Excitement because the Access course I had done to enable me to get here had only whetted my appetite; the fear, on the other hand, tended to overcome the excitement. I was afraid I would not be able to reach the standard of work expected; I was afraid I would not be able to contribute anything in seminars; I was afraid I would not understand the lectures.'

(Diane Nutt in Arksey, H., Marchant, I. and Simmill, C.
(1994) *Juggling for a Degree*)

Many mature applicants to any form of education feel they are not qualified for acceptance and therefore lack personal confidence. Even those who have been accepted often continue to feel unsure of themselves and, initially at least, live in awe of the other students. In so doing, mature applicants tend to undervalue the skills and disciplines learnt in their daily lives at home and in the workplace, and to underestimate the relevance of their accumulated life experiences. You should find it a useful exercise, then, to examine your own strengths. The questions below are designed to act as a 'trigger' for that process:

- What have I learnt from running a home?
- What have I learnt from bringing up children?
- Have I learnt to be organised in my work?
- Have I developed self-discipline at home and/or at work?
- What writing skills do I have?
- Do I enjoy discussing issues with other people?
- What are my interests? Why am I interested in them?
- Have I learnt to work as part of a team?
- Have I learnt to work independently?
- Do I have the ability to adapt and change as circumstances demand?

Once you have done this, it is a good idea to list the skills that you have, whatever field they might be in. Quite apart from helping you realise the extent of your potential, this can also be a useful preparation for when you apply to do a course.

WHAT DIFFICULTIES WILL YOU FACE AT HOME?

'My parents really supported me. They encouraged me and had my little girl two days a week.'

(Dawn, graduate 1999)

'When I was in full-time employment my partner used to ask me about my work: "How was it going?" "What was I doing?" Since I have been to university he has not asked. He has stated he is not interested in academic arguments as he lives in "the real world" and I do not.'

(Arksey, H., Marchant, I. and Simmill, C. (1994) *Juggling for a Degree*, p. 16)

'I feel our relationship would not have been so interesting if I had not attended university.'

(Arksey, H., Marchant, I. and Simmill, C. (1994) *Juggling for a Degree*, p. 16)

Many mature students and their families have to make sacrifices during the time they are in education. Because some courses presuppose a significant amount of private study, the normal family and social routines can be affected, particularly when the student is studying full time. As a result, relationships can be affected, and are sometimes even put under strain.

'Education will offer you many cultural and social opportunities, and these will open new horizons but, on the downside, may also cause some conflicts of interest. In my family for example, we have evolved what is called "Mum's 100 minutes", which occurs three days a week, after the six o'clock news. This is when I can get a clear run at my college work, uninterrupted by husband or children. It is a mobile phone-free zone and my daughter, bless her, even turns down her Spice Girls CDs! However it has changed our social life which, in the main, used to revolve around seeing two particular couples – pubs, meals out, cinema, that sort of thing, which is partly on hold because of my studies.'

(Rebecca, adult returner in her 30s, quoted in *The Mature Student's Guide to Higher Education* 2000)

The majority of mature students and their families overcome any problems that may arise, and declare that it has all been worthwhile once the certificate has been gained or the graduation photograph is safely installed on the sideboard! However, it is important to recognise that entering education is often to take on a major commitment and that the process of gaining the qualification is long and can be arduous. It only makes sense, then, to assess the level of support you would receive or opposition you would encounter from within your family, and to consider seriously whether your existing responsibilities would permit you to take on such a very large new commitment. Some relevant questions you might ask yourself are:

- How would your partner react to your becoming a student?
- How would the rest of your family and your friends react?
- Could you cope with your children if you were on a full-time course?
- Could you support yourself financially?
- Could your family manage without your current earnings?
- How much time would you spend travelling to your proposed course?

> 'I realised that I would be gambling with my own self-esteem and that my friends may judge me on the outcome. I am particularly aware of the interests of my former workmates, who in the majority supported me, but I have a gut feeling that one or two are slightly envious of me and resent the fact that I am getting a chance to better myself'.
>
> (Coare, P. and Thomson, A. (1996)
> *Through the Joy of Learning. Diary of 1,000 Adult Learners*, p.23)

However positive you may feel the reactions of those who are important to you may be, you are strongly advised to discuss the possible impact of your studies on your lifestyle and your domestic arrangements. The diary of a student given at the end of this chapter could provide a useful basis for a realistic discussion of possible changes in your family life.

HOW WILL STUDY AFFECT YOU?

Some students study at home on their own by 'distance learning' or correspondence course, for instance with the National Extension College or the Open University (see Useful Contacts). But for most becoming a student means entering a new social situation and encountering many new people. The majority of mature students, after perhaps a few initial doubts and worries, flourish in their new setting. But it is worthwhile considering questions about the new relationships into which you will be entering and the new activities you will be engaged in as a student. You might like to consider the following questions:

- How would you feel about being identified as a student by your local community?
- Do you enjoy participating in discussions and arguments?
- How do you react to criticism?
- How would you feel about working on your own a great deal?
- How would you feel about being responsible to yourself, and yourself only, for the amount and quality of the work you do?
- Would you find it difficult to organise your own study timetable?
- How would you feel about spending a lot of time with people who are in general younger than yourself?
- How would you feel about being taught by tutors who may be younger than you?
- How would you feel about spending a lot of time reading?
- How did you react to the last major change in your life?
- You might change as a result of becoming a student. How would you feel about this?

'People say I've changed, the way I think, the way I articulate ideas. I question things more. Its broadened my outlook on life. I question my parents' views a lot to myself. I look at things objectively now.'

(Gill, graduate 2000)

Thinking through these and similar questions that are relevant to your situation should help you begin to assess in a realistic and honest way your life, your abilities and what becoming a student might entail. It is possible that some of the questions are difficult to answer at the moment, particularly if you have been out of education for a long time.

HOW WILL IT ENHANCE YOUR CAREER?

'I'll be disappointed if I can't find the kind of job I want after I leave but I don't expect to walk into a job.'

'To be honest, I don't think I would advise anyone with a good job to give it up for university; once you're out of the job market, things change so fast it is hard to get back in. However if you're like me and have been out for a while with children, then it's a great way to get back into things.'

(Arksey, H., Marchant, I. and Simmill, C.
(1994) *Juggling for a Degree*, p.48)

'I did it to satisfy something in myself. Not to lead into an occupation.'

(Dawn, graduate 1999)

Many mature students find that their experience in education enriches their lives in all sorts of ways that they would not have anticipated. Unfortunately some also discover that their expectations of immediate career opportunities with their new qualifications prove to be exaggerated. If career ambitions are your principal motivation in wanting to further your education, you are strongly advised to seek advice from careers offices, potential employers, etc. It is also wise to check that your chosen career is an area of employment which is open to people of your age. You can then ensure that the course you propose to do is appropriate for that type of work, and find out whether you will have to undertake any further training.

Some courses are directly relevant to a career aim, such as law, nursing, librarianship, hairdressing, computing and accountancy, but others may be of only limited value to a specific career goal. You may get some general information about career prospects from college or university prospectuses, but if you want specific information about careers you may need to contact your local careers office. There are also booklets available on a variety of careers such as those published by AGCAS (Association of Graduate Careers Advisory Services) that outline the academic requirements for particular careers. These should be available in all higher education careers services and many careers offices (see also Books and other resources at the back of this book). Another publication worth consulting is *The Penguin Careers Guide*, which as well as giving details of the necessary qualifications for various careers also lists the number of women and older entrants in those areas of employment.

Other students of all ages embark on courses without any particular career consideration in mind. A common experience for many students is that they find their experiences as they progress through their studies generate interests that crystallise into specific career aims.

Many employers are more interested in applicants who have studied in any subject rather than just those who have done specific courses, so although careers considerations may be important it may be equally desirable to apply for a course that you are likely to enjoy and do well in than to worry unduly about career considerations too early. It would be folly to believe that a degree or diploma in any one subject rather than another would be a passport to success or a gateway into a particular career. It is also important to be aware of the fact that, with few exceptions, careers, or jobs 'for life', no longer exist as they did in the past; in future people will have a wider range of careers and work experiences during their working lives.

Diary of a part-time student on an NHS Operating Department Practitioner diploma course, 2001

06:00   Get up – the early start means that my daughter and I can eat breakfast together before I leave.

06:50   Leave house to catch the bus to the station.

07:20   Arrive at the station. Get coffee to wake me up and newspaper (one of our lecturers always asks what articles are of relevance to our course).

07:35   Catch train. Have a good chat with other students – our main chance to catch up with each other.

08:35   Arrive and walk to university.

09:00   Lectures start.

12:15   Lunch hour – we have something to eat and then start on what is a futile search for books on the reading list. This is extremely frustrating because I cannot come back until next week. I must find a local source for books (my university library does not have an exchange scheme with the one I go to).

13:15   Rush back for afternoon lectures.

16:30   Cross town to get train home.

18:00   Arrive home. Change bags and go straight out again – my daughter is a St. John's cadet and we have a meeting on my university day.

18:45   Buy sausage roll – my dinner!

20:30 Thank goodness somebody has offered us a lift home!
21:00 Home.
21:20 Bed.
21:30 Asleep!

Chapter 3
QUALIFICATIONS AND PREPARATION

This chapter deals mainly with the qualifications you need for entry into higher education and how to get those qualifications. If you are already qualified to enter higher education (see below), but feel that you would like to dip your toe into the water before you take the plunge, there are also suggestions as to how you can achieve this. However, before doing this it is also important to look at other courses you might be interested in. For the vast majority of FE courses, adult education classes and evening classes all you need to do is enrol before a specified date, if there are spaces available in the class you can join. For some courses such as A-level classes you may be required to have a relevant GCSE, but not always. For admission to an Access to Higher Education course you are likely to be asked to a short informal interview and possibly to write something. Admission to Open University courses is, as the name implies, 'open'. This includes admission to degree courses.

ARE YOU QUALIFIED FOR HIGHER EDUCATION?

Admission to all other higher education courses usually implies having some qualifications or work experience. Mature applicants to universities and colleges of higher education usually fit into one of four categories:

■ those with academic qualifications;
■ those who hold professional qualifications;
■ those who have directly relevant work experience but no formal qualifications;
■ those who have no qualifications or directly relevant work experience.

23

Although these divisions are usually distinct, it is conceivable that you will fit into more than one of them. Each of the categories will be considered in turn together with the various courses of action that are available to you.

Educational attainments and achievements at work

A-levels or equivalent Universities and colleges usually require a minimum of two A-levels (or equivalent, eg BTEC, Scottish Highers, etc) before applicants are considered for a place on a degree course; or one A-level for a Higher National Diploma (HND). All full-time entrants to higher education courses are administered by a central agency, the Universities and Colleges Admissions Service (UCAS), and not by individual universities or colleges (see Chapter 4). Nevertheless it is always worth checking with the admissions office of the institution you are interested in if your qualifications differ: they may be taken into account. However, there are some courses where admission is only by limited discretion on the part of the institution. Teaching, for instance, is a popular choice among older applicants but you need to bear in mind before you apply for entry that you must have certain GCSEs.

Standard entry applicants (those who enter higher education directly from school) are usually required not just to pass their exams, but also to get specific grades in them. If you passed your exams some time ago this requirement may not be applied as rigorously; instead your experience and motivation will determine whether or not you are accepted, at least in part. If, however, you have only recently acquired your qualifications, you may have to conform to the same standards as the standard entry applicants. Again, check with the admissions officer as it very much depends on your chosen course of study. Remember, qualifying for entry does not necessarily guarantee you a place.

Sometimes mature applicants have already had some experience of higher education when they make their applications. It might be that you have already acquired some formal qualification such as HND or one or more credits with the Open University. If you are in this situation you may well find that these qualifications make you eligible for a place on the course you are interested in (but see the next paragraph), or even enable you to gain direct entry into the second or third year of the course. A significant minority of mature students are returning to higher education after having made a 'false start' in higher education at some earlier time. If you are in this situation you may find your previous learning will be acknowledged when you are considered for a place, and it is unlikely that you will be discriminated against because of your earlier withdrawal.

Even if you satisfy the average entrance requirements, though, this will not make you eligible for acceptance on every course in any one institution. You need to check carefully whether you will need a specific qualification to gain entry on to the course you are interested in. For degree courses, you are likely to find that physical science departments (chemistry, physics, medicine, engineering, mathematics, etc) are unable to accept students with as broad a range of academic qualifications as those providing courses in the humanities (philosophy, literature, history, etc), the arts and the social sciences. This is not to say that all science courses demand higher grades though; in fact often the opposite is true. The entrance requirements for courses can be found in *Degree Course Offers* (see Books and other resources) or under the departmental entries in the prospectuses. If you have any doubts concerning your eligibility contact the admissions tutor of the department concerned or the admissions officer or registrar of the university or college.

If you find that a specific additional qualification is required to make you eligible for the course you want to join it is wise to ensure that any preliminary studies you undertake will be acceptable before you start them. Again, admissions officers should be happy to give you guidance on this.

Vocational qualifications Many mature applicants gain entry to higher education on the strength of vocational qualifications they have obtained since leaving school. One student, for instance, applied with an ONC in civil engineering, and was accepted unconditionally on a social sciences degree course:

> 'It was difficult at first. I wasn't prepared for the way the college was organised ... but okay regarding academic demands. Essays were hard work at first, and I expected a more formal teaching structure.'

If you have such a qualification – for instance in nursing, City & Guilds, etc – it is worth checking to see if this will qualify for entry to a degree course. There is no guarantee that it will, for some institutions are willing to accept such qualifications and others are not. The prospectus of the institution you are interested in may not give specific details of its policy here; if so, do not assume that there is no such policy, but contact the admissions staff. This is best done by letter to the appropriate department, for it is unlikely that a considered reply can be given instantly, particularly if your qualification is relatively obscure or, possibly, has been superseded by another one in its field. Give as much information as you can, including syllabus details and any official documentation if possible. Make it clear what course you are interested in. You may even find that your qualification will entitle you to remission for some of the course, for instance by 'skipping' the first year.

No formal qualifications but related work experience Some of those who aspire to enter higher education are in the apparently difficult situation of having accumulated knowledge and developed skills through their work experiences without acquiring any paper qualifications to prove it. Until comparatively recently such learning was unrecognised by universities and colleges, mainly because of the difficulties of assessing it. Now, though, many institutions are at last properly acknowledging such knowledge and skills, and considering them as a valid qualification for acceptance. This process is known as the Accreditation of Prior Experiential Learning (APEL) and this is where credit is given for your work or voluntary experience. Some institutions offer an APEL module to help you assemble evidence of such learning.

No formal qualifications or relevant work experience Many mature students in higher education began the entry procedure with no qualifications to their name. If you are in this situation, there are a number of options open to you or preparatory courses you can take.

Sometimes universities and colleges are prepared to interview 'unqualified' applicants if they have demonstrated their suitability for the course on the UCAS application form. They may even offer you a place and waive the need for any further qualifications if they believe that you are sufficiently motivated and capable of doing the course.

> 'Nothing is written in tablets of stone; there are as many routes in as there are students. Two favourite examples are that of a friend who was accepted on the strength of her interview alone, without having studied anything at all for 15 years; and that of another friend who was

accepted on to a postgraduate course without being a graduate or having undergone any kind of further education. In both cases work experience was the deciding factor which gained them admittance to university.'

(Arksey, H., Marchant, I. and Simmill, C.
(1994) *Juggling for a Degree*)

WHICH COURSES OR EXAMS WILL HELP YOU QUALIFY?

'Access was extremely good preparation ... an enormous confidence booster ... I had to work very hard, but I coped.'

(Student (and ex-shop assistant),
now studying for a degree in social policy)

Access courses

These courses are now probably the most popular means of entering higher education for prospective students who have no qualifications. They offer people who have been out of education the opportunity to acquire study skills and further their knowledge in a particular area of study. One student, for example, who is now training to be a teacher, had been working as a fitter before starting an Access course:

'It showed me how to write essays and do note-taking and that kind of thing ... I got an introduction to teaching and design ... I still wasn't sure whether it would be enough for when I got into college, but it has been.'

The time commitment for Access courses varies from one or two sessions per week (often available in the evening) over two years, to full-time courses over one year. The courses can offer a very supportive environment, help you face such challenges as writing essays, preparing projects and sitting exams, and filling in your application form for higher education. However, you should bear in mind that the amount of contact time inevitably influences the content of the course. As a general rule of thumb, the less time you have in the classroom, the less ground you can cover. It is important, therefore, that you try to assess your own needs and select an Access course that will satisfy them. At the same time it may be necessary to consider the commitment required for a full-time course. This is what one student had to say:

> 'It swallowed evenings – there was lots of contact time … no time during the day to study because of the time spent in lectures.'

Some Access courses may be held in colleges that have a franchise or affiliated relationship with a neighbouring institution of higher education; passing the course may mean a guarantee of an interview, or even a place, at that institution in some cases. These arrangements are relatively rare, though, and most Access courses act as a general 'currency', making you eligible for a variety of higher education courses but not guaranteeing a place on any one of them. Access courses are certified by validating bodies which ensure that standards are shared and maintained across the country. Such courses are given a 'kitemark' and are recognised by most universities and colleges. However, it is important to note that passing an Access course does not necessarily qualify you for entrance to all courses in all institutions of higher education.

Access courses are usually held in local colleges of further education. To find out about the courses that are being run in your area, contact your local college (they can be found under 'Schools and Colleges' in the Yellow Pages), or go to your local library, careers service or education advice centre, if there is one near you. Alternatively, if you intend to apply to a higher education institution locally, they may well be able to give you advice on such courses. Even if you decide not to go on to more study from an Access course the learning experience is still worthwhile in itself and there are many gains from studying on such a course.

Entrance exams

> 'I'd always wanted to teach, but missed the chance when I was 18 …
> We couldn't afford to lose any of my pay before I started at college …
> so taking an entrance exam was the only possible way in for me.'
> (Male student and former lorry driver, aged 40)

In some institutions you may be required to sit an entrance exam of some kind. These tests vary from course to course and from institution to institution.

This method of entry does have its drawbacks, though. Even if you pass the entrance exam, you may well find the first few weeks of study a struggle. If you have not been in education for some time you may not have had the opportunity to develop the study skills that others have. One woman student, for instance, was made redundant from her job as an accounts administrator. Because she would have had to wait an extra year to get on to an Access course, she did an entrance exam instead:

> 'I was disadvantaged by not doing Access as far as studying was concerned ... there were problems focusing on the subject matter of essays ... But I would rather be at college than lose a year on Access.'

Most mature students are able to catch up with the other students who have entered through alternative routes, however.

The quality that universities and colleges are looking for is potential for higher education. However, if you feel unsure of how you would perform in an entrance exam, or are apprehensive about doing it (as most people are), you are strongly recommended to do some preparation for the exam. Sometimes short preparatory courses are available before the exam is taken but, if not, there are a number of practical books available to help you. Such books may be consulted in your local library, and they all contain standard 'tips' and advice. Two that are particularly recommended are: *Exams Without Anxiety* by David Acres, and *The Good Study Guide* published by Open University Press (see Books and other resources). You can also usually obtain copies of the entrance exam papers from previous years by contacting the institution concerned. This will give you a good idea of what kind of test it will be and the kind of questions you will be asked, and let you prepare accordingly. Try to 'psyche yourself up' into a positive frame of mind; everybody can do well in exams if they believe they can succeed. University and college prospectuses usually indicate which departments select on the basis of these tests.

Foundation courses

> 'At the onset of the Foundation programme the mere thought of writing an essay would have filled me with terror – but I have now returned my fourth essay for assessment – a measure of my progress so far.'

Some institutions now have what are known as Foundation courses. These may form part of a specific degree course and can extend to the first year of that course. You may not need any qualifications to be eligible for entry on to a Foundation course, and if you pass it you are automatically allowed to proceed to the subsequent years of the course. Foundation courses can also act as a preliminary introductory year to a specific degree course. Passing a Foundation course does not entitle you to entry to any course other than the one it is designed for, however.

Sometimes the first year or foundation year of a course is 'franchised' out to another institution such as a college of further education. This may mean that you can do part of your degree at a more local institution and only have to face the inconvenience of travelling or moving in the latter part of the course.

Open University credits

When you have completed a year of Open University you are awarded a credit. (You need six credits for an ordinary degree.) These are frequently used by mature applicants as a qualification for entry to degree courses. Sometimes former Open University students who have more than one credit are given 'remission' from some courses, so that they are able to start at the beginning of the second year of a degree course, for example. You do not require any qualifications to be eligible for entry on to an Open University course but sometimes you do have to wait a year before you can start. The advantage of doing such a course as a way of qualifying is that the Open University is totally geared to the needs of older students who can participate without any significant disruption to their normal lives. All studying can be done by 'distance learning' – correspondence, television and radio (although there is some opportunity to meet other students and your tutor later on).

The disadvantage with using the Open University as a means of gaining entry into higher education is that, because many institutions require two credits, the process of gaining these qualifications usually takes two years as opposed to the one year for Access or A-level (or equivalent).

Taking A-levels (or equivalent)

You can study for A-levels (or Scottish Highers and other equivalent exams) full time, part time, during the day or in the evening, either at your local college of further education or through correspondence courses such as those run by the National Extension College. In addition, some schools are now encouraging adults to attend their A-level courses alongside the 16 to 18-year-olds. Some universities and colleges will consider BTEC courses as equivalent to A-levels; these are also taught at local further education colleges. You can find out about the availability of such courses in your area through local schools, colleges or libraries.

Such courses will provide you with a qualification that is recognised by all universities and colleges and will prepare you for higher education in a number of ways. Furthermore, some higher education courses still specifically demand qualification at A-level (or equivalent) for all applicants, since a certain level and type of knowledge is required to be able to cope with the courses from the outset. The disadvantage of taking A-levels (or equivalent) for mature applicants is that they are usually attempting to study in a year courses that are designed to be studied over two years. As a result, the teaching can be somewhat rushed, and the time available for reading around the subject is restricted. Nonetheless, people who have been out of education for some time seem to enjoy studying on such courses, and manage to fit it in with other demands on their time such as work and running a home.

Vocational A-levels

Previously known as advanced GNVQs (General National Vocational Qualifications), these are administered by the Edexcel Foundation (formerly the Business and Technology Education Council (BTEC)) and are courses which have the same value as conventional A-levels but that have a distinctly work-related bias. There is a considerable range of subject areas among the 13 courses available (at the time of writing), including art and design, manufacturing, business, science, information and communication technology and health and social care. There is more assessed course work and fewer exams than is the case with conventional A-levels, a feature that may appeal to many older students.

Residential diploma courses

There are a small number of colleges that offer residential courses to adults who have no previous qualifications. These courses usually last one or two years, and are widely accepted as entry qualifications for higher education. They offer the chance for a complete break from your present lifestyle and provide the opportunity to give your full attention to studying. Financial support may be available through a bursary from the Department for Education and Employment. If you are interested, apply to the individual colleges.

OTHER WAYS TO PREPARE FOR STUDY

Even if you do have the necessary qualifications to enter higher education, you may well feel that you need to limber up your intellectual 'muscles' before you have to face up to the rigours of your chosen course. Some people do this by attending an Access course; however, other options exist that are less demanding on your time.

Self-preparation

You may well not have the time or the money to prepare yourself for higher education by doing another course. Even if you already have the necessary qualifications you may feel understandably anxious about how you will cope when you get there and would like to help yourself in some way. There are many books on study skills or returning to study usually available in local libraries, or that are relatively inexpensive to buy. You can also contact the institution you are hoping to go to and ask for a reading list for prospective students. They may send you a list intended specifically for people who are due to start the course shortly, or alternatively the first year reading list. Even if your local library does not have the books in stock they can usually order them for you although a fee may be charged for this service. It is even possible to join the library of your local college or university in some cases, on an independent basis. An enquiry may prove worthwhile if they are likely to have the relevant resources for loan or reference.

You may prefer to do this kind of preparation once you have secured a place, but reading some relevant books can also be a sound investment when you are called to interview. Being asked about a book you have recently read is quite common, so reading something well known or recently published, or that has received some acclaim, is an excellent idea for nearly all prospective students.

Study skills courses

These courses are often run as part of an adult education programme by local education authorities or university continuing education departments. They offer preparation for higher education through practice in time management, essay writing, note-taking and seminar participation – all necessary skills on degree programmes. Taking a study skills course should therefore help you to feel more confident about entering higher education as well as helping you to study efficiently. Such courses are also available by correspondence and although you do not get the opportunity to meet other prospective students, they do give you greater flexibility in fitting the course into your own time schedule and other responsibilities, and are especially valuable if travelling presents problems. Some people also prefer the anonymity of correspondence courses; you can ask the tutor whatever you want without fear of embarrassment in front of a class, secure in the knowledge that you will never meet the tutor!

Leisure-oriented classes

Some prospective students like to begin studying again by taking an evening class, just to warm themselves up. There are a great variety of such classes available in the day or evening: among the ever-present cake decorating and car maintenance classes it is usually possible to find courses that can provide the right atmosphere in which to prepare for entry into full-time study (though there is rarely much opportunity to gain experience of study skills such as essay writing or examinations). Such classes tend to be in the humanities and social sciences, however; prospective students who want to do physical sciences or develop their study skills might find it more profitable to do a GCSE or BTEC course.

GCSEs and other assessed courses

Many prospective students find it useful to attend one of the many GCSE courses that are available in most areas. Some students, particularly those who intend to go into teaching, may have to register for GCSE courses in English language and mathematics if they do not already have them, to be eligible for entry in any case. Others might want to gain some grounding in a subject that they propose to study but of which they have as yet little experience. A GCSE course may be more demanding than a more leisure-oriented class, but it does enable you to get back into studying in a relatively painless and interesting way, and may convince the institution to which you are applying that you mean business. Alternatives to GCSEs are BTECs, and the newer GNVQ courses are available in a range of subjects and skills.

Computer courses

If you are thinking of attending a formal course, particularly in higher education, basic computing skills will definitely be a bonus. You may well be expected to word process your assignments, and the Internet will be an invaluable tool in your research. If you don't have a 12-year-old son or daughter to teach you there are many inexpensive or free courses available at all sorts of locations. Check your local careers advisory service, library or education advice centre for details. If you already have some computing experience, a course in touch-typing, some of which can be obtained on CD-ROM, will be a great time saver. All the government and educational organisations and most institutions publish huge amounts of information about courses and facilities on the Internet, so it will also be useful in making your application.

> 'When I started my course I knew virtually nothing about IT. I would strongly advise anyone thinking about study to gain at least basic skills if possible before you start. It gives you one less thing you have to learn in the early days.'
>
> (Part-time student on Operating Department Practitioner diploma course)

Associate student schemes

Increasingly colleges and universities are opening up a variety of their courses to the general public. You can attend classes alongside regular students; in some cases your work is assessed, in others it is not. Although you do normally have to pay to participate on one of these schemes, it is an ideal way to get a realistic idea of what student life is like. Although you can do such a course as a 'one off' you may find that you can use any credit you gain on it towards a qualification if you decide to go on studying at that institution.

A final thought

Of course, even if you do have the necessary qualifications at the grades required, there is no guarantee that you will be offered a place: the decision is entirely at the discretion of the institution concerned. You may receive offers of places from a number of institutions, but get turned down by the one that was your favourite. This simply reflects the fact that places in higher education are in short supply and does not necessarily say anything about your qualifications. It is possible that you will be turned down even if you have the formal qualifications because of other factors – an interview or your application may be the deciding criterion. If you do get turned down, you can try to find out why by contacting the admissions staff (or the mature students adviser if there is one) and you may be told, for example, that your A-level grades were not high enough. This may sometimes indicate whether you can remedy the situation in any way and apply again the following year. Applicants who are confined to a limited number of institutions may find this a useful step to consider.

Chapter 4
CHOOSING A COURSE IN HIGHER EDUCATION

This chapter is entirely concerned with the complicated process of applying to do a course in higher education. The process for applying to other adult education courses is much more straightforward (see previous chapter).

If you intend to apply for a full-time or sandwich degree course the application process is made in the vast majority of cases through UCAS. The UCAS handbook and application form are available from FE colleges and careers offices, education advice centres or by contacting UCAS directly (the address and website address are listed under Useful contacts at the back of this book). If you want to study part time at a university or college you should apply directly to the institution.

Applications for Higher National Diploma (HND) courses or full-time Higher National Certificate (HNC) courses are also made directly to UCAS and not to the institutions where they are taught. More general information on HNDs and HNCs is available from the institutions, educational advice centres, careers offices or from the Edexcel Foundation.

A glance at the UCAS handbook suggests a bewildering array of choices in higher education. There are currently 42,000 courses on offer at 261 institutions. In its 500+ pages there are literally thousands of course entries at different institutions of higher education. It starts with the University of Aberdeen and ends with the University of York and the courses offered range from divinity through east Mediterranean studies and maritime engineering to radio studies and prosthetics! If you are trying to choose a course the task appears daunting in the extreme. You are allowed up to six choices on the UCAS application form – how do you make a selection from such a vast and intimidating offering?

In practice, of course, the range of choices available to each individual applicant is much more manageable and you will only be concerned with a fraction of the courses listed. In fact the major considerations for many mature applicants are those that relate to accommodating their future studies into their existing lives. Factors that frequently affect mature students' choice of course and institution are therefore:

- Where to study?
- How to study?
- What to study?
- What are your personal needs and tastes?
- Any other considerations?

GEOGRAPHICAL CONSIDERATIONS

'I felt lost and lonely, living in. I was the only mature student in my block and other students were apprehensive of me – I was the only bloke on the corridor. My wife couldn't stop over at weekends and it was difficult to keep in touch with the kids.'

Many older applicants are constrained geographically, placing some limitations on where they can apply. Some applicants with children, for example, cannot travel far and consequently there may be only one or two institutions that are realistic propositions for them. Factors that you may need to bear in mind are:

- Are you confined to your locality?
- Can you travel daily?
- How far is acceptable?
- Could you live away from home during the week?
- Could you live away from home during the term?
- Could you move to a new locality altogether?

It may well be that you can undertake a certain amount of travel but are not able to move away from your home. In this case it is worthwhile looking at a map of all the institutions in your area, some of which you may not be aware of. Although people living in or near the larger metropolitan areas would seem to have a greater choice of universities and colleges this need not necessarily give them all the advantages. The accessibility of such places is in practice often dependent on travel facilities; a decent train service can make somewhere 40 miles distant a possibility, but if you have to rely on an infrequent bus service a comparatively short distance may be a nightmare. If you are limited by such considerations and it means there are only a small number of institutions to which you can apply, don't worry. Once you have worked out which ones are realistic possibilities, you can then choose a course from what they offer, bearing in mind certain other factors that should be considered, as follows.

HOW (AND WHAT) TO STUDY

Distance learning – the Open University

If it is simply not feasible for you to attend an institution on a daily basis, this is no reason to give up the idea of applying for higher education. Distance learning gives you the opportunity to study and gain recognised qualifications via correspondence courses, the most popular of which is the Open University.

There is a wide variety of courses available, and a wide variety of people study with the Open University. Obtaining an ordinary OU degree usually involves study over a period of six years. Credits are gained each year by passing a course with a prescribed number of assessments and final examination. The study material for each course is divided into units and is sent by post. There are also television and radio programmes, computer software and cassette tapes available to supplement the written material. Assessments (normally essays) are undertaken and sent back to a tutor (assigned to each student) who comments very fully on them. Everybody starts with a Foundation course and then progresses to courses of different levels of difficulty. As some students prefer to work in a group rather than alone it is possible to make social contacts at a local study centre. There is also some face-to-face teaching for all courses, varying from weekly tutorials for Foundation courses to occasional weekend study sessions and week-long summer schools. Students are encouraged to form self-help groups and all students are allocated a tutor who also acts as an individual counsellor.

The OU is one higher education institution set up specifically for adult learners and so is totally geared to the needs of such a group. Many students find it a welcoming and relaxing atmosphere in which to fit their learning and other commitments. Each area of the UK has been divided into regions, each of which has an Open University Regional Centre. You can find out about your region and other details by writing to the Students Enquiry Service at The Open University (see Useful contacts). Other universities and colleges are also providing opportunities for students to study at least some of their course 'at a distance'.

Higher National Diplomas (HNDs)

Many mature students choose to study for Higher National Diplomas that are designed to equip people for particular areas of employment. These courses normally last two years, and are taught in universities, colleges of higher education and some colleges of further education. They provide students with a huge range of academic and work-related skills, some of which are listed below:

Business studies	Graphic design
Information technology	Leisure studies
Media production	Social care

Qualifications for entry The minimum entry requirement for an HND course is normally one A-level (two Scottish Highers, BTEC National Diploma or equivalent). Mature students are also accepted if they have successfully completed an appropriate Access course or, occasionally, if they have particularly relevant work experience.

From HND to degree The HND qualification is fully recognised in its own right by employers, but after successfully completing an HND it is possible (with some exceptions) to transfer to a degree course. You can enter the final year of a closely related degree programme, gain direct entry into the second year of a related degree programme, or use your HND as an entry qualification into the first year of a completely unrelated degree. One-year conversion courses are available at some institutions to upgrade HNDs to a degree qualification.

Part-time degrees

Many institutions offer a range of higher education courses part time. Birkbeck College, for example, one of the constituent colleges of London University, offers all of its degree courses on a part-time basis. Other universities and colleges are offering an increasing number of such courses with similarly more flexible structures. They either form part of a whole programme of part-time courses, which may for example be run in the evenings, or it may be possible to follow the same courses as full-time undergraduates, but taking fewer units in a given time period.

OTHER FACTORS

Special needs support

> 'I enjoy being successful on the course. I work harder than other students because of my disability and have to work on an on-and-off basis.'

Students with disabilities are one of the social groups traditionally under-represented in higher education (though it is difficult to estimate the exact proportion since calculation of numbers depends on the criteria used to define 'disability' and also relies on students declaring their special learning needs). Students with disabilities of all kinds currently study successfully at all levels of education. There is a variety of support available for those who need it, which includes specially adapted accommodation, personal assistance, computer-aided technology, note-takers, BSL translators, hearing loops, etc. The needs of people with mental health difficulties of all kinds are now being recognised and addressed by educational institutions.

Changes in the law have led to more enlightened policies and support to disabled students. Many colleges and universities now employ disability coordinators who help to provide appropriate support to those who require it. Despite this, some institutions are still developing their services and may still have much to learn. Thus if you are disabled, you are advised to contact all the institutions you wish to study at, indicating the nature and implications of your disability and any special arrangements you may need regarding your studies, daily living and accommodation. Although many applicants find it very hard to make a special case for themselves in this way it will be easier for you and for everybody else if arrangements are in place before you start your course, particularly as you will have plenty to cope with when you arrive in any case!

Skill – the National Bureau for Students with Disabilities – is an organisation that provides information and advice to disabled students as well as applicants to further and higher education. It publishes booklets on funding for disabled students and applying for education.

Other considerations when selecting a course

Methods of assessment If you are not good at exams there may be courses available that are assessed in other ways, at least for part of the course. Consider carefully what type of degree you want to do and where.

> 'I was limited in my choice of university by my husband's work; moving house was not an option. Fortunately the local university had a modular course that was perfect for me. I could build up good marks from course work alone and reduce the pressure during exams (which I hate almost as much as spiders and housework). This is the first tactic – if you hate exams look for course work-based courses; if you hate course work look for exam-dominated courses. You know your own preferences so don't be pressured into applying for a course you know won't suit you.'
>
> (S. Anderton (1998) *How I got my First Class Degree*, p.68)

Combined or single subject degrees You may be more comfortable doing a degree in more than one subject, especially if you are uncertain about what you are good at or are unclear as to your interests. You can combine subjects now in a variety of ways: by combining two subjects equally; a major/minor combination in which one subject predominates; a multi-subject course; or a modular course that is drawn from a variety of courses or even subjects.

Work experience/sandwich courses Some institutions provide work experience as part of the degree programme. This can form a large part of the course – a year in the case of sandwich courses (although sometimes students have the option of whether or not to do the sandwich element). There may also be a number of compulsory courses that are work related in some way, or there might be opportunities to acquire work experience or short vocational courses of which you can take advantage. Mature students need to be clear about whether they want to do such courses. Some really want to get off the treadmill of work for a short period. If you feel like this you need to assess very carefully the amount of time allocated to more vocational work and avoid such courses if you think that they will spoil your academic experience. On the other hand you may welcome such opportunities and think that they could be useful to your future career, or interesting and challenging in themselves. It is then worthwhile to see which institutions offer these opportunities.

Other considerations when selecting a university or college

It is obviously impossible to give more than very general guidelines about what to look out for in the courses you are considering. What seems important is to try to discover as much detailed knowledge as possible about the institutions you have chosen and to realise that, unfortunately, however carefully you make your choice, it is ultimately the institution that chooses you rather than the other way around!

The place in which you study is of key importance and will largely determine the quality of the experience you will enjoy there. The appendix contains a list of the higher education institutions in the UK. The availability of childcare facilities or special study support services are instances of the kinds of amenities that might make you decide in favour of one institution rather than another. Having some idea of the proportion of mature students at each place is also helpful. Most mature students attend their local institution of higher education, but if you want to move away, the availability and cost of accommodation may be an important factor in your decision. There are three main possibilities:

■ Single standard university accommodation, which is usually available for all first year students but may be unsuitable for some older students.
■ Renting accommodation privately; the college or university should have a list of such accommodation.

■ An increasing number of institutions are making specific provision for mature students and their families.

These are factors which it is possible to measure; there are others that are unquantifiable but at least as important. The atmosphere of the institution, the friendliness of staff and students and the physical setting are all elements that may be felt differently by individual students but are significant in the overall experience of the institution. Such aspects cannot really be judged from prospectuses, and it is advisable to visit the institution and talk to other students to get a better feeling of the general ambience of the place. Most universities and colleges offer open days that will enable you to visit them. UCAS publishes free of charge a booklet, *University and College Open Days, Pre-taster Courses, and Education Conventions*, giving details of such events.

A final postscript should perhaps be added to this section: once you have been accepted by an institution there is usually some flexibility if you find that you have selected the wrong course. This is not to say that you shouldn't consider your choices very carefully, but it is worth bearing in mind that they are not always irreversible.

Chapter 5
APPLYING TO UNIVERSITY OR COLLEGE

THE UCAS APPLICATION PROCEDURE

1. **Contact UCAS** to obtain an application form, the UCAS handbook, and a copy of *The Mature Student's Guide to Higher Education*. These are also available from education advice centres and careers services and are free of charge. If you are currently on a further education course these will be available to you through the college.
2. **The UCAS handbook** contains every course available at all the institutions of higher education in the UK. It also lists the UCAS codes for these institutions and individual course codes, which you will need when you fill in the application form. The handbook should be read alongside the prospectus of each institution you are interested in. It also contains the addresses of institutions should you need to contact them for more information or prospectuses.
3. **The UCAS application form** is accompanied by a section-by-section instruction leaflet. Read it carefully! It explains how you, as a mature student, should answer the questions. The most sensible thing to do is to make a photocopy of the application form and to practise on that before you fill in the real thing.
4. You can **choose up to six courses** in your application, but if you only wish to make one choice this is perfectly acceptable. Each choice should be made on a separate line, and you should give the institution and course code of each selection. You can choose more than one course at any individual institution, and/or course(s) from more than one institution on the application form.
5. **Referee** The instruction leaflet does give a few suggestions as to who you should select as your referee – employer, careers officer, colleague, etc. However, current practice suggests that higher

education institutions often prefer referees who can make an informed comment on your academic and intellectual potential. This is not always easy – not all mature applicants have been in employment recently, and not all employers can make valid judgements on such matters. If you are doing an Access or other preparatory course you are best advised to choose your tutor even though he or she may not know you well when you make your application. In that case, ask your tutor to mention in the reference that they will be prepared to give an update closer to the time you are interviewed. Again, if you have done some other course recently, ask the tutor to act as your referee. Maybe you know a teacher, or have done unpaid work with, for instance, a school or voluntary organisation – all of these are possibilities. Your choice of referee can be important so if you have problems get in touch with the mature students' adviser at the institution you are interested in. Check that your referee knows all relevant details about you. If you are applying to only one institution and have been told that you do not have to provide a reference you should simply indicate this.

6. The section to really work on is the '**Personal statement**'. This gives you an opportunity to sell yourself, to explain your background and your reasons for wanting to enter higher education. Include any information that might make you stand out from other applicants, and which could act as a 'trigger' for the interviewer to ask questions if you are called for interview. There is no magic formula for completing this section, but the following suggestions may be helpful:

   ■ Reading a page of densely packed detail about lives well spent can become monotonous: younger applicants have always spent their time doing good deeds, playing sport and, of course, being dedicated to their studies. Your application needs to contain something original.

   ■ Humour or a sense or irony is usually appreciated by the reader. One applicant who worked in a packing factory prior to starting an Access course described how he used to speak to the boxes through sheer boredom. And many mature students, for example, can describe light-heartedly their sense of house arrest as a result of looking after a couple of pre-school children!

- Think about dividing the section into headings: reasons for wanting to study the course, paid or unpaid work, hobbies, etc.
- Describe the skills you have gained from your life experiences (see Chapter 2). For instance, one woman wrote about the skills learnt from being a single mother, including effective time management.
- It may be a good idea to explain why you finished with education before and why you now wish to take it up again. This is especially useful if you have previously embarked upon higher education and withdrawn for some reason.
- Try to be specific about your interests. This gives the reader a better idea of you as a person, and provides some material with which you are familiar for an interviewer to question you on. So, rather than state that you 'enjoy reading', as many applicants do, say what type of books interest you – for instance, women's writing or science fiction.
- UCAS suggests mentioning career aspirations, but if you do not have a particular goal in this area, don't worry. You can say either that you don't have any special ambitions at this stage, or leave it out altogether.
- If you can describe any academic interests, particular questions that interest you, and what led to these interests, this will almost certainly capture the attention of the reader.
- There are many trite and meaningless phrases that continually recur in applications. Never say you 'like people' on your application form or, indeed, at your interview!
- Remember that what you write on your application form is likely to form the basis of at least part of your interview, so do check that you write with this in mind and anticipate some of the questions to which your statements may give rise. On the other hand, you should also remember you may not get called for an interview so the application form is your only chance to 'sell yourself'.

7. Finally a few basic but important tips:

- Applications can be submitted from September onwards in the year before you intend to begin your studies. **Send off your application as early as possible** – UCAS operates on a 'first come, first served' basis. If your application is late (after mid-December) don't be put off – you still stand a chance, but not necessarily on the course of your choice.

- **Write in black ink** -the form has to be photocopied.
- **Write legibly** – remember that the form will be reduced when photocopied, so if your writing is naturally small, write larger than normal.
- **Spell correctly** – check words like 'psychology'!
- **Complete and stamp the acknowledgement card.**
- **Include payment.**
- **Keep a photocopy** of the application for your personal use – it's often invaluable to know precisely what you have said about yourself when you go for interview!
- **Referee** – Remember that it is your responsibility to pass on your completed application form, acknowledgement card and fee to the referee. He or she then fills in the reference section and sends the application on to UCAS.

'I encourage our mature students to use positive action words to describe their own experiences. This is particularly (but not exclusively) important for vocational courses; words such as 'produced/observed/analysed/discussed' reinforce you as an individual who can critically evaluate your experiences. You then need to match this to your chosen institutions' general course requirements ... Look to make an effective use of key linking sentences such as 'Having taken part in ... Has enabled me to'. In doing so you should have a personal statement that is coherent, comprehensive and organised'.

(*The Mature Student's Guide to Higher Education 2001*).

PREPARING FOR THE INTERVIEW

Many institutions no longer interview applicants who are applying directly from school but sometimes interview mature candidates. As a result, some months after you have sent off your application form, usually some time between November and March, you may be invited to go along for an interview. Although you may wish to avoid thinking about it at all, it is definitely important to be prepared. There is no simple formula for success, of course, but thinking constructively about your interview will make the whole prospect less daunting and enable you to equip yourself well and, who knows, even have an enjoyable experience!

Before you go to the interview there are certain things you can do to prepare yourself:

1. **Re-read the photocopy** of your UCAS form. This is most important as frequently interviewers will have a copy to hand at the interview, using it as a source of information about you for their questions. You may be able to anticipate the most likely questions that your application form will provoke. Nothing looks more foolish than saying to an interviewer 'Did I really say that?' when they quote something you have written on the application form!

2. **Re-read the prospectus**. You may have applied for up to six different courses at six different institutions. When you go for interview, you need to convince the interviewer that you really want to study at that institution – you won't be taken seriously otherwise. So check that the details of the course and institution are fresh in your mind.

3. **Are you familiar with the subject matter?** Especially if you are doing a subject that you have not studied before, make sure that you can define what the subject is and have a reasonable idea of the kinds of questions you would be addressing on the course. Detailed academic knowledge, however, is not expected at this stage.

4. **Do you know where you are going?** Some institutions are spread over a variety of sites and campuses, sometimes miles apart. You don't want to turn up for your interview and find that you are on the wrong campus! If you are in any doubt about where you should go, phone the university or college for information. Most will be able to send you directions and/or a map. If you have to travel a long distance for the interview, you may be offered overnight accommodation, in which case you will have more time to find out where everything is.

5. **Clothing**. When questioned about their worries about the interview process, many applicants mentioned their uncertainty about what they should wear. In practice, applicants wear a variety of things to interviews, from jeans and sweatshirts to three-piece suits. The best advice is to wear what you feel comfortable in and, if in doubt, err on the conservative side. This is not the time for experimenting with the latest or most outrageous fashion. It may be sensible to look as if you have made an effort, even if the academic interviewing you looks in need of a handout from a charity. Remember that you may be travelling a long way to your interview, so don't wear anything that gets crumpled too easily.

6. **Consider what qualities universities are looking for** in their applicants. In contrast to the precise job descriptions provided by many employers, higher education institutions have often been vague about the qualities and skills they value highly in applicants. Individual interviewers, even in the same department, might emphasise abilities differently, and in any case will all rely to some extent on 'gut feeling'. More recently, however, many institutions have attempted to be systematic in their approach to interviewing procedures and are more explicit about what qualities they are looking for, describing them in prospectuses, etc. When asked which factors influence their assessment of interviewees, admissions tutors usually list the following:

   ■ **Motivation** – evidence of interest in and a commitment to the subject.
   ■ **Relevant work, domestic or leisure experience** – and an appreciation of how it relates to the proposed studies.
   ■ **Ability to communicate** – expressing yourself effectively in writing and in speech, the willingness to listen, and a readiness to work in groups.
   ■ **Organisational skills** – whether it be the ordering of ideas and tasks or time management.
   ■ **'Potential'** – evidence of recent achievement, for instance on an Access course or other preparatory course; signs of initiative and imagination; above all, self-confidence.

   At this stage the interviewer is not looking for detailed knowledge of the subject area or specific academic skills.

7. **You may find a rehearsal helpful.** Some applicants find that thinking through responses to probable questions and actually verbalising those responses to another person are completely different experiences. If you can practise with another person ask them to think of questions of their own – they might hit on that vital question which you failed to anticipate. Some teachers encourage practice interviews with students interviewing each other: it is amazing how much nervousness is generated by the exercise. Ask for honest feedback, not forgetting your non-verbal communication. You should try to meet the gaze of the interviewer, although you can look away to think. Try to keep your limbs still, don't fiddle, and don't cover your mouth with your hand! If you don't have someone to rehearse with a mirror may be better than nothing at all.

THE INTERVIEW

The frame of mind with which you enter the interview room is as important, if not more so, than any of the practical steps you can take to prepare for the interview. Immediately prior to your interview it is a very useful exercise to take a positive look at yourself, to assess your strengths, and to remind yourself why you would be a good person to be offered a university or college place. It is a good idea to write these points down to fix them in your mind. People are often diffident about their abilities and tend to dwell on shortcomings. Nevertheless, when mature students have been asked to name strengths that students direct from school may lack, the lists are usually very impressive. The 18-year-olds may enter higher education with very good A-levels and many of the academic study skills that mature students are still uncertain about. What they often lack, though, are those life skills related to independent living, which are new to them but not to mature students, accustomed to organising their lives, to working on their own initiative and, perhaps, not least, getting out of bed in the morning!

The interview may be preceded by an introductory chat to all interviewees or alternatively you may be shown directly to the interview room. Interviewers will expect you to be apprehensive and will make allowances – so don't worry if you are, as most applicants tend to be nervous. You may be interviewed by two people, but it will usually be only one. At the start of the interview a standard part of the introductory procedure is to shake hands, so be ready for it and do so with a good, firm grasp. Wait to be offered a seat before you sit down – these will help give a positive impression from the start. The interviewer may try to put you at ease and may ask you to 'Say a little bit about yourself.' Do have a response to this question ready and don't say 'There's really not a lot to tell!' Also, don't worry about hesitating before you respond to a question – try and think out your answer first and you are less likely to tie yourself in knots.

Likely questions

- Why do you want to study for a degree/diploma now?
- Why do you want to study biology/dance – whatever else you have chosen?

- Why do you want to study at this particular institution?
- You may be asked about your paid work experiences.
- You may be asked about your previous studying experiences. If you are currently on a course you will almost certainly be asked about it. If you are doing a project on the course, you will usually be asked to talk about that, too.
- You may be asked about your career aspirations.
- You may be asked about a book you have read recently.
- You may be asked about some current affairs issues, especially if you have applied to do a related subject, such as politics, social policy, etc.
- You may be asked about any other institutions you have applied to.

If you can talk at reasonable length about these matters it means that you can keep a certain level of control over the interview and, furthermore, if you can suggest other areas for questions this can make the whole process much easier. For instance, if you have taken an Access course, prepare a description of it but invite the interviewer to ask you more about a particular aspect of the course. 'Sociology is my favourite module and I am finding the work on the family particularly interesting' would be one way of doing this. With a few tactics like this, in no time at all the interviewer will be saying how much he or she has enjoyed meeting you, but that the time has run out.

Difficult questions One of the most common fears that applicants have is not understanding the question. You can ask the interviewer to repeat a question, but if you are certain you don't know it's much simpler to say 'I don't know' or 'I'm afraid I haven't been introduced to that topic' than to flounder.

Any questions? Eventually the interviewer will indicate that the interview is drawing to a close and will ask the inevitable 'Are there any questions you would like to ask?' Prepare for this in advance, but make sure your question hasn't already been covered in the interview or in the prospectus. Try to show that you are familiar with the course description in the prospectus when you put your questions. Obviously you may ask whatever you want but some useful examples are:

- What proportion of mature students have you had on the course in the past?
- How well have such students done?

- How is the course assessed? (If this is not in the prospectus.)
- Could you tell me a little more about how work placements are organised?
- Is timetabling organised in such a way as to fit in with the needs of student parents?

Questionable questions You should not be asked questions that could be construed as likely to form the basis of discrimination against you. Questions such as 'What does your husband think of you doing this course?' or 'How would you cope with your children while you are here?' are unacceptable. Responses you can make are:

- I don't think this is very relevant and I would rather not answer the question.
- Are there answers that may be used against me?
- I have coped with similar challenges before.

No one can anticipate all eventualities, but most interviewers will do their best to encourage you, to put you at ease, and to be fair-minded in their assessment of you. Nevertheless, it has to be said that the experience of interviews is variable, and it is often difficult to assess how well you have done. Sometimes the interview is so informal that you can end up thinking that the interviewer is obviously not going to offer you a place or you would have been asked more searching questions. On the other hand you may be uncertain as to how well you have done because you feel that you have failed to answer some questions adequately. If you have other interviews to attend use each completed interview as a learning experience; it is always worthwhile reviewing how you performed, and considering how you can improve on your responses.

OFFERS FROM UCAS

After the interview, you will probably hear from UCAS within about three weeks. You are able to hold two offers under the present UCAS system. There are three possibilities:

- **Unconditional offers.** This means that the institution is happy to admit you on the basis of what you currently have to offer. If you accept the offer you must go there.

■ **Conditional offers**. This means that the institution will accept you if you obtain certain qualifications, eg successful completion of an Access course. You can only accept one conditional offer firmly; this means that if you meet the requirements you must go there.

■ **Insurance offers**. You can hold one other offer as insurance for if you fail to meet the conditions of the conditional offer. This will impose lower requirements than the conditional offer. If you do not meet the conditions of the conditional offer, but meet the conditions of the insurance offer, you must go there.

You will need to reflect carefully on what you have seen of the institutions that have made you offers to determine how they meet your needs (which may, of course, have changed since you filled in the original application form).

If you are not made an offer you are strongly recommended to approach other institutions *before* the Clearing process begins in late August to see if they are interested in your application. Clearing is a particularly frantic time for admissions tutors, and you are less likely to receive individual attention once it has started than if you apply in advance.

THE CLEARING PROCESS – IF INITIAL PLANS FAIL

Clearing refers to the UCAS procedure by which applicants who have not been offered a place (or who have failed to get their grades) can try to find one on a course where there are still vacancies. This is more likely to have a successful outcome if you are free to go anywhere, rather than if you are restricted geographically. The process starts in late August or early September after the A-level results have been released and after UCAS has confirmed places for those students who have obtained the grades required of them.

To participate in the clearing process you need a Clearing Entry Form (CEF) which is issued by UCAS when you become eligible for clearing (ie when you have not been offered a place on any of your chosen courses or when you have failed to reach the specified grades). Lists of courses that still have places are made widely available – at local careers services, on the UCAS website and in the quality press. You should look at these lists and assess the available courses in the same way you did with your original choices, using the appropriate prospectuses. Once you have decided on a possible course phone or visit the institution and have a chat with the admissions tutor. At this stage all offers are informal and may only become a definite commitment once the Clearing Entry Form is in the hands of the admissions tutor. Try not to be panicked into accepting a place on what might turn out to be an unsuitable course; you may need to reassess what you should do at this stage.

Chapter 6
FINANCIAL ISSUES

'Save money if possible from the first and second years from employment so you don't have to work in the final year.'

'When I gave up work my spending capacity reduced. I was used to quite a high standard of living, but now I'm living on an overdraft and have had to sell my car.'

Finance is a continual worry for students of all ages. Many mature students re-enter education with significant financial commitments, and making ends meet can become a major problem. Most students have to take paid work in order to maintain an acceptable income during their studies. It is therefore important that you have an accurate idea of what your level of income is likely to be before you embark on your studies, and discuss the practical implications with those around you who may also be affected.

There are two main costs that higher education students have to cope with – tuition fees and living expenses.

Tuition fees

Most **full-time** mature students who have not been in higher education before are exempt from paying tuition fees if they fulfil one of the criteria below:

■ If you are over 25 at the beginning of the academic year.
■ You have been married for at least two years at the beginning of the academic year.
■ You have been in full-time employment and/or were in receipt of a state benefit during the three years prior to the beginning of the academic year.

The tuition fee is paid direct to the higher education institution by the Student Loans Company. Details on how to apply for this support are outlined below.

Part-time students are eligible for non-repayable assistance towards the cost of their tuition fees if they have not been in higher education before and they fulfil one of the criteria below:

- You are on state benefits.
- You are on a low income and receive tax credits.

You should apply direct to the higher education institution you plan to study at to receive this support.

Full-time and part-time students who wish to study in a Scottish university or college of higher education are exempt from tuition charges.

Living costs

Student loans The days of student grants are long gone, so most students have to rely on student loans in order to meet their living expenses while in higher education. These loans are administered by the Student Loans Company, which was specifically set up for this purpose when student grants were abolished. Loans are repayable after completion of studies once you are in employment and earning more than £10,000 per year. Repayments are calculated as a percentage of your income on a sliding scale, so that if you earn £12,000 you pay 1.5 per cent, if you earn £15,000 you pay 3 per cent and if you earn £20,000 you pay 4.5 per cent.

To be eligible for a student loan you must be under 55, and if aged between 50 and 54 you must indicate your intention of returning to work after you graduate.

Full-time students studying outside London can currently borrow up to £3815 per year, while those studying in London are eligible for up to £4700.

Part-time students can borrow up to £500 per year at the time of writing. Eligibility is determined by your income, your partner's income, and whether you have any children.

Applying for financial support

■ Obtain form HE1 (Application for Higher Education Support) from your local education authority (LEA), by contacting the Department for Education and Employment (DfEE) helpline directly on 0800 731 9133, or the DfEE website www.dfee.gov.uk/studentsupport.
■ Return the completed form to your LEA not more than four months after the start of the academic year (October), and ideally well in advance of it.
■ The LEA will then send you form HE2, which asks detailed questions about your financial position.

If you live in Scotland you should apply to the Students Awards Agency for Scotland (SAAS) and if you live in Northern Ireland you should apply to the Department of Higher and Further Education Training and Employment (see Useful contacts).

Other sources of financial support for students in higher education

Dependants' grant If you are a single parent, or have dependant adults in your family, and are studying full time, you may be entitled to a dependants' grant. At the time of writing, this stands at a maximum per year of £2175 for the first child and up to £1740 for each other dependant child. The grant is paid with the student loan, but is not repayable.

Lone parents' grant This is a grant paid to single parents who are in full-time studies. At the time of writing it is worth up to £1075. The grant is paid with the student loan, but is not repayable.You cannot claim both the lone parents' grant and the childcare grant (see below).

Other grants for students with dependant children

Childcare grant Full-time students with children are eligible for up to £100 a week assistance towards the cost of childcare for the first child or £150 for two or more children. You cannot claim both the childcare grant and the lone parents' grant (see above).

School meals grant If you are entitled to the dependants' grant you may be eligible for up to £250 for each primary school child and £270 for each secondary school child.

Travel, books and equipment grant This grant is available to full-time students with dependant children, and is worth up to £500.

These grants are paid with the student loan, but are not repayable.

Disabled students' allowances If you are disabled you are eligible for financial support to cover the cost of special equipment necessary for you to carry out your studies and/or a non-medical helper.

Access bursaries The Access fund was established to provide for students who experience severe financial hardship. Each university or college is allocated a fixed amount that it is responsible for distributing. Parents studying full time can apply for up to £500 to their university or college for help towards the cost of child care, so long as they are not receiving the lone parents' grant (see above). These payments are not repayable.

Hardship fund Support is available through the university or college to provide for students who experience severe financial hardship. Anything between £100 and £3500 can be made available, sometimes as a non-repayable grant, sometimes as a loan. The circumstances under which payments are made and the amount that is paid out are entirely the responsibility of the institution, and all hardship funds are under enormous pressure. Students may receive help towards a variety of expenses such as high rents, childcare and medical expenses.

Career Development Loans If you plan to taken a vocational (work-related) course but are not eligible for funding through your LEA you may be able to obtain a Career Development Loan, which is administered through the DfEE. You can apply for loans between £300 and £8000 for courses that can last up to two years (or three years if they include work experience). Repayment of the loan begins one month after the end of the course. To apply for a Career Development Loan contact the CDL Information Line (0800 585 505).

Housing benefit Students in higher and further education are entitled to housing benefit if they are lone parents and/or receive certain state benefits or tax credits. The amount you receive will be based on your 'nominal income', which not only includes your actual income, but also the full amount of the student loan to which you are entitled, whether or not you have borrowed that much. This is an area that is constantly subject to change, so it is wise to consult your local housing benefit office on the support you will be entitled to.

Charities, trusts and foundations There are a number of educational charities that sometimes help mature students. There are a variety of registers of such charities that are available in most reference sections of your local library. Example are the *Grants Register*, published by Macmillan, and the *Educational Grants Directory*, published by the Directory of Social Change. There is not a lot of money available from such sources and some target specific groups, which range from people who have certain disabilities or who live in a particular area, to Polish immigrants or the sons of Methodist ministers! Charities exist largely to give *additional* help, so they are usually most sympathetic if you have run into sudden problems due to unforeseen circumstances: for instance the non-payment of maintenance by an ex-husband, or bereavement. They will want to check that you have already applied for assistance through the normal channels. Charities maintain good lines of communication between each other to guard against those who might be tempted to make multiple claims to a number of funds.

Sponsorship Employers are always on the lookout for promising future graduate recruits, and are prepared to invest in a limited number of undergraduates through sponsorship. Sponsored students are required to sign a contract that usually obliges them to undertake periods of training with the organisation during the academic year and to work for them for about eight weeks during the summer vacation and of course to work for them after graduation for a specified period. In return you receive an income for the academic year, and are paid a normal salary for the time you work in the holidays. Most sponsorship deals are offered to students in the sciences, technology, engineering and business. Sometimes organisations are quite specific about the courses and institutions that they are prepared to sponsor. Many advertise their sponsorship packages in careers services; alternatively, a variety of guides exist, one of which is *Students Support Sponsorship Funding Directory*, published by CRAC/Hobsons, which is also available in most careers services and public libraries. It may also be worth exploring the possibility of arranging a sponsorship deal with your current employer, if you have one – they might be prepared to help. Sponsorships are usually, but not always, set up before you begin your studies, so if you are interested in the idea it is sensible to waste no time in contacting potential companies.

Finance for Open University students The Open University provides some help to those of its students who are reliant on benefits, and operates its own hardship fund. You can make a claim for financial help at the same time as you apply for a place on a course. If you are successful you may get all the fees and expenses paid for the course. A student loans system operated by the Open University is under consideration at the time of writing.

Health professional courses NHS bursaries are available for all full-time or part-time students on courses such as nursing, midwifery and radiography. Tuition fees are paid in full by the NHS, and there is also a maintenance grant of £4805 available to students studying outside London. Both degree and diplomA-level students may receive an extra allowance if they are over 26, have dependants, are single parents or have to pay extra costs while on a clinical placement. These allowances are non-repayable.

Financing preparatory courses for higher education

A-levels If you do a part-time A-level course at an adult education centre or college of further education you will have to pay the course fee. However, most LEAs have a policy of waiving these fees if you are in receipt of state benefits or disabled, or at least only make a nominal charge.

Correspondence courses If you are studying by correspondence you are responsible for the payment of the fees, although it may be worthwhile getting in touch with your local education authority to see if they will help with some of the costs. Some educational charities may be sympathetic, too.

Access courses Access courses in most parts of the country are free. Many Access courses are organised so that attendance time does not exceed 16 hours in any one week. This means that if you are reliant on benefits you maintain your eligibility to those benefits.

Foundation courses If you have been accepted on a Foundation course for a university or college degree it counts as part of your degree entitlement and applies whether the foundation year is called Year 0 or Year 1, and whether the course is held at the institution itself or at another location. It is funded in the same way as the higher education programme.

'Return to Learn' courses You may well have to pay the fees for these courses, although fees may be reduced or waived if you are reliant on state benefits.

Where to find advice

The Department for Education and Employment (DfEE) publishes a booklet entitled *Financial Support for Higher Education Students.* This details the sources of financial support available and the steps you need to take to obtain it. Copies are available from careers services or you can contact the DfEE information line or website.

Local education authorities (LEAs) publish booklets containing up-to-date, detailed information on financial support to students. They can also give advice over the phone, although they usually prefer it if you can write to them with your enquiry. The phone number and address of your LEA will be available from the local library, education advice centres or careers service, or in the phone directory under the name of the local council.

Benefits Agency Your local Benefits Agency office can give you individual advice on your eligibility for benefits. Although many students have been effectively removed from the welfare system some important groups are still eligible for help. You can also phone Freephone 0800 666555 for confidential advice.

Higher education institutions Financial advice is available within most universities and colleges, from advisers employed by the institutions or who work for the Students' Union. The adviser can often help you ensure that you take advantage of all sources of funding that may be available to you.

Advice agencies such as the Citizens Advice Bureau or local authority welfare benefits units are always a valuable source of information.

STUDENT FINANCE – THE BRIGHTER SIDE

'Debts! ... If I had known what the economic situation would be I would not have come. But I don't regret having come. The sacrifice will have been worth it.'

The information given in this chapter presents an unvarnished account of the financial situation you may well have to cope with if you enter higher education. Many institutions have 'job-shops' that advertise local part-time jobs. Many concessions are made available to students in a variety of ways: students are exempt from paying Council Tax (subject to certain conditions), and are eligible for free or reduced-cost dental and optical care. Many shops, cinemas, theatres, leisure centres, etc make reduced charges to students, and all full-time students can obtain a discount on rail fares. There are insurance and travel companies that provide services exclusively for students. And most universities and colleges have a range of shops, canteens and bars on campus that sell goods at lower prices than on the high street. So although things are not going to be easy, they will be a lot better than they could be!

Chapter 7
A FINAL WORD ... WHEN YOU GET THERE

Re-entering education is a major change for all older students. Anxiety and a lack of confidence are common feelings. However, many mature students have an easier time than school leavers, who are often separated from their friends and away from home for the first time in their lives. Although many worry about fitting in with younger students, this is in reality rarely a problem and indeed mixing with other students of all ages is very positive for all concerned.

'As a mature student I enjoyed mixing with such a large age group and have never really felt I was an "oldie". I hope that my age and life experiences benefited the younger students I mixed with too.'
(Julie, graduate 2000, *A Guide for Mature Students,*
College of Ripon and York)

'Although I was thrilled to be here and slotted in easily, I was also incredulous – I expected somebody to come up and say "Sorry, it was all a mistake – you shouldn't be here".'

And virtually all mature students lack confidence in their academic ability, and seem to assume that the younger students will be more capable. Gradually this assumption is replaced by the realisation that they have many advantages:

'You will do well at university if you have made a conscious decision that studying is what you would rather be doing ... for the three years that you are there, instead of just ending up there because that's what everybody does after their A-levels or you don't fancy a job. This perhaps explains why mature students often fare better. I went to university after five years in the workplace, not only had I got the usual fresher preoccupations – losing my virginity, getting blasted on cheap booze, coping without mum doing the cooking and washing, etc – out of the way, I had no doubt that studying would be, for me, a luxury rather than a chore.'

(Ruth Adams in Tolmie, P. (1998)
How I got my First Class Degree, p.51)

'If somebody had said to me I would be doing an Access course I would have laughed … I have battled against feelings of lack of confidence and insecurity … I have thought back to when I was at school and wondered whether I am capable of learning again after a break of what seems like an aeon.'

(Coare, P. and Thomson, A. (1996)
Through the Joy of Learning. Diary of 1000 Adult Learners)

Your confidence develops, and as the college or university becomes more familiar and you make social contacts you feel free to enjoy your new life:

'I was very fortunate during my degree to find some very good friends. We tended to work together and support each other. This was a real blessing. We could borrow notes from each other if needed, more importantly we could talk to each other. As they say, three brain cells are better than one. Meetings over coffee often shed light on topics and clarified points that we might have missed on our own. My degree owes much to my friends.'

(S. Anderton in Tolmie, P. (1998)
How I got my First Class Degree, p.69)

'Now for the first time since I came to England, I feel I belong to something. People are like me, eager to learn and improve every day.'

(Liliana Fiorento in Coare, P. and Thomson, A. (1996)
Through the Joy of Learning. Diary of 1000 Adult Learners)

The majority of students find that their experiences in education lead to changes in the way they see themselves, others and the world around them:

'In some ways it's been the hardest thing I've ever done. The easiest thing would have been to give up. But I couldn't have lived with myself. It was partly for my daughters. If you have a degree you have some status. It gives you inner confidence.'

(Angela, third year undergraduate 2000)

'I've changed from a passive housewife to a more self-confident, assertive, self-considering individual.'

'Others see me as a more understanding person ... better at communicating things, arguing points and providing evidence to support my argument.'

Sometimes students come to see their family and friends in a different light:

'I take my parents less for granted now – I have more time to think about what they have done for me.'

'I'm catching up with some of my friends in terms of achievement – I feel more equal.'

'I realise now that my family expected me to be their doormat – to be what they wanted me to be, and I probably let them do it.'

Finally, when asked what they had gained from re-entering education overall, some mature students gave the following replies:

'Besides being relaxing and enjoyable, my partner and I also realise we're more observant of and appreciate more of the things around us. We look at things differently now. We enjoy and gain far more out of paintings, literature and architecture. Even TV programmes have an extra dimension. So I thank God for the chance to return to learning. I feel like a sponge that's been squeezed dry and is now opening out through the joy of learning.'

(Bernard in Coare, P. and Thomson, A. (1996)
Through the Joy of Learning. Diary of 1000 Adult Learners).

'Doing a degree made me look at things more deeply. I could look at some of the questions I had raised with myself when I was working with women before I came to college.'

(Dawn, graduate 1999)

'I now have more self-assurance ... I have some intelligence – having left school at 14 gave me the feeling of not being bright.'

'I now look at the world in a totally different way ... I've met others from different walks of life and I have wider horizons. I feel fulfilled and have much more emotional security.'

APPENDIX

LIST OF UNIVERSITIES AND COLLEGES

There are many sources of information available to help you research the opportunities in continuing and higher education. Below is a list of all providers of higher education courses. Some of these are organisations that supply only a comparatively small number of higher education courses. All of these institutions will issue a free annual prospectus giving details of courses, student facilities and details of how to apply. The prospectuses are usually also available in formats accessible to the disabled such as braille, large print, audio tapes, etc.

Most institutions have extensive websites that contain much more detailed information than the prospectuses, and have the benefit of being up to date. If you do not have Internet access, most libraries have this facility with staff to help and there are also Internet cafés, of course.

Most of the numbers given below are those of the admissions offices, but there may be other staff you would like to contact, such as the mature students adviser, disability advisers and accommodation officer. Don't be afraid to ask!

A tick for childcare provision indicates that there is some on-site provision. The provision varies greatly and may not be available on all sites and may only be available for certain ages of children. However, even where there is no provision this does not mean that there is no help available. Some institutions provide substantial financial help which would enable you to place your child in a nursery of your choice. All nursery places are in high demand so we would advise making early contact with any nursery.

Institution	Website	Telephone	Percentage of mature students	Childcare
Aberdeen University	www.abdn.ac.uk/sras	01224 273504	15	✓
Abertay Dundee University	www.abertay.ac.uk	01382 308080	20	✗
Aberystwyth, University of Wales	www.aber.ac.uk	01970 622021	9	✓
Anglia Polytechnic University	www.apu.ac.uk	01223 363271	23	✓
Askham Bryan College	www.askham-bryan.ac.uk	01904 772211	48	✓
Aston University	www.aston.ac.uk	0121 359 6313	6	✓
Aylesbury College	www.aylesbury.ac.uk	01296 588588	n/a	✓
Bangor, University of Wales	www.bangor.ac.uk	01248 382017	15	✓
Barking College	www.barking-coll.ac.uk	01708 770000	26	✓
Barnsley College	www.barnsley.ac.uk	01226 216171	27	✓
Basford Hall College, Nottingham	www.ncn.ac.uk	0115 916 2001	76	✓
Basingstoke College of Technology	www.bcot.ac.uk	01256 354141	n/a	✓
Bath Spa University College	www.bath.ac.uk	01225 323019	7	✓
Bath University	www.bathspa.ac.uk	01225 875875	29	✓
Bell College of Technology	www.bell.ac.uk	01698 283100	21	✗
Birmingham College of Food, Tourism and Creative Studies	www.bham.ac.uk	0121 414 3344	5	✓
Birmingham University	www.bcftcs.ac.uk	0121 604 1000	13	✓
Bishop Burton College	www.bishopb-college.ac.uk	01964 553000	20	✗
Bishop Grosseteste College	www.bgc.ac.uk	01522 527347	21	✗
Blackburn College	www.blackburn.ac.uk	01254 55144	37	✓
Blackpool and The Fylde College	www.blackpool.ac.uk	01253 352352	31	✓

Institution	Website	Telephone	Percentage of mature students	Childcare
Bolton Institute of Higher Education	www.bolton.ac.uk	01204 528851	21	✗
Boston College	www.boston.ac.uk	01205 365701	n/a	✓
Bournemouth University	www.bournemouth.ac.uk	01202 524111	15	✓
Bournemouth, Arts Institute at	www.arts-inst-bournemouth.ac.uk	01202 533011	17	✓
Bradford College	www.bradford.ac.uk	01274 233081	16	✓
Bradford University	www.bradfordcollege.ac.uk	01274 753241	33	✓
Bretton Hall	www.bretton.ac.uk	01924 830261	17	✓
Bridgwater College	www.bridgwater.ac.uk	01278 441234	n/a	✓
Brighton University	www.brighton.ac.uk	01273 600900	24	✓
Bristol University	www.bris.ac.uk	0117 928 9000	5	✓
Bristol, UWE	www.uwe.ac.uk	0117 3443333	16	✓
British School of Osteopathy	www.brunel.ac.uk	01895 203214	15	n/a
Brockenhurst College	www.bso.ac.uk	020 7407 0222	66	n/a
Broxtowe College, Nottingham	www.brock.ac.uk	01590 625549	n/a	✓
Brunel University	www.broxtowe.ac.uk	0115 917 5252	n/a	✗
Buckingham University	www.bcuc.ac.uk	01494 522141	10	✗
Buckinghamshire Chilterns University College	www.buckingham.ac.uk	01280 814080	37	✗
Burton College	www.burton-college.ac.uk	01283 494411	n/a	✓
Cambridge University	www.cam.ac.uk	01223 333308	3	✓
Cannington College	www.cannington.ac.uk	01278 655123	n/a	✓

Institution	Website	Telephone	Percentage of mature students	Childcare
Canterbury Christ Church University College	www.cant.ac.uk	01227 782490	20	✓
Canterbury College	www.cant-col.ac.uk	01227 811188	n/a	✓
Cardiff University	www.cardiff.ac.uk	029 20 874404	7	✓
UWIC, Cardiff	www.uwic.ac.uk	029 2041 6070	15	✓
Carmarthenshire College	www.ccta.ac.uk	01554 748000	40	✓
Carshalton College	www.carshalton.ac.uk	0208 770 6800	n/a	✓
Central England University in Birmingham	www.uce.ac.uk	0121 331 5000	19	✓
Central Lancashire University	www.uclan.ac.uk	01772 201201	19	✓
Central School of Speech and Drama	www.cssd.ac.uk	020 7722 8183	26	✗
Chelmsford College	www.chelmcollege.u-net.com	01245 265611	n/a	✓
Cheltenham & Gloucester College of Higher Education	www.chelt.ac.uk	01242 532825	17	✓
Chester	www.chester.ac.uk	01244 375444	11	✓
Chesterfield College	www.chesterfield.ac.uk	01246 500562	21	✓
Chichester College of Arts, Science and Technology	www.chichester.ac.uk	01243 536196	n/a	✓
Chichester University College	www.ucc.ac.uk	01243 816002	21	✓

Institution	Website	Telephone	Percentage of mature students	Childcare
City College, Birmingham	www.ccm.ac.uk	0121 236 4725	53	✓
City College, Manchester	www.candi.ac.uk	0161 957 1790	37	✓
City and Islington College	www.candi.ac.uk	020 7700 9200	n/a	n/a
City of Bristol College	www.cityofbristol.ac.uk	0117 904 5000	34	✓
City of Sunderland College	www.citysun.ac.uk	0191 511 6201	n/a	✓
City University	www.city.ac.uk	0207 040 5060	17	n/a
Clarendon College, Nottingham	www.ncn.ac.uk	0115 960 7201	27	✓
Cleveland College of Art and Design	www.ccad.ac.uk	01642 288888	24	✗
Colchester Institute	www.colch-inst.ac.uk	01206 518000	27	✓
Cordwainers College	www.cordwainers.ac.uk	020 8985 0273	45	n/a
Cornwall College with Duchy College	www.cornwall.ac.uk	01209 611611	38	✓
Courtauld Institute of Art	www.courtauld.ac.uk	020 7848 2645	12	n/a
Coventry Technical College	www.covcollege.ac.uk	024 7652 6700	n/a	✗
Coventry University	www.coventry.ac.uk	024 7688 7688	14	✓
Cranfield University	www.rmcs.cranfield.ac.uk	01793 785400	17	✓
Crawley College	www.crawley-college.ac.uk	01293 442205	44	✗
Croydon College	www.croydon.ac.uk	020 8686 5700	38	✗
Cumbria College of Art and Design	www.cumbriacad.ac.uk	01228 400300	20	✗
Darlington College of Technology	www.darlington.ac.uk	01325 503050	n/a	✓
Dartington College of Arts	www.dartington.ac.uk	01803 862224	31	✗

Institution	Website	Telephone	Percentage of mature students	Childcare
Dearne Valley College	www.dearne-coll.ac.uk	01709 513101	n/a	✓
De Montfort University	www.dmu.ac.uk	0116 255 1551	15	✓
Derby University	www.derby.ac.uk	01332 622222	21	✓
Dewsbury College	www.dewsbury.ac.uk	01924 436229	19	✓
Doncaster College	www.don.ac.uk	01302 553610	27	✓
Dudley College of Technology	www.dudleycol.ac.uk	01384 363277/6	33	✓
Dundee University	www.dundee.ac.uk	01382 344160	15	✓
Durham University	www.dur.ac.uk	0191 374 2000	8	✓
East Anglia University	www.uea.ac.uk	01603 456161	13	✓
East Durham & Houghall Community College	www.edhcc.ac.uk	0191 518 2000	n/a	✓
East London University	www.uel.ac.uk	020 8223 2835	42	✓
Easton College	www.easton-college.ac.uk	01603 731200	n/a	✗
East Surrey College	www.esc.org.uk	01737 766137	78	n/a
Edge Hill College of Higher Education	www.edgehill.ac.uk	01695 584274	21	✓
Edinburgh University	www.ed.ac.uk	0131 650 1000	9	✓
Enniskillen College of Agriculture	www.enniskillencollege.ac.uk	01365 344853	13	✗
Essex University	www.essex.ac.uk	01206 873666	12	✓
Exeter College	www.exe-coll.ac.uk/higher	01392 205581	26	✓
Exeter University	www.ex.ac.uk	01392 263035	8	✓

Institution	Website	Telephone	Percentage of mature students	Childcare
Falmouth College of Arts	www.falmouth.ac.uk	01326 211077	24	✓
Fareham College	www.fareham.ac.uk	01329 815200	n/a	✓
Farnborough College of Technology	www.farn-ct.ac.uk	01252 407028	13	✓
Glamorgan Centre for Art and Design Technology	www.gcadt.ac.uk	01443 663309	19	✗
Glamorgan University	www.glam.ac.uk	01443 480480	16	✓
Glasgow University	www.gla.ac.uk	0141 330 4575	11	✓
Glasgow Caledonian University	www.caledonian.ac.uk	0141 331 3000	22	✓
Gloucestershire College of Arts and Technology	www.goldsmiths.ac.uk	01452 426549	36	✓
Goldsmiths College	www.goldsmiths.ac.uk	020 7919 7282	30	✓
Greenmount and Enniskillen Colleges	www.greenmount.ac.uk	028 94 426700	n/a	n/a
Greenwich School of Management	www.greenwich-college.ac.uk	020 8516 7800	47	✗
Greenwich University	www.gre.ac.uk	020 8331 8590	28	✓
Grimsby College	www.grimsby.ac.uk	01472 311222	n/a	✓
Guildford College of Further and Higher Education	www.guildford.ac.uk	01483 448500	n/a	✓
Halesowen College	www.halesowen.ac.uk	0121 550 1451	n/a	✓
Halton College	www.haltoncollege.ac.uk	0151 423 1391	40	✓
Hammersmith & West London College	www.hwlc.ac.uk	020 8741 1688	n/a	✓
Harper Adams University College	www.harper-adams.ac.uk	01952 815000	6	✗

Institution	Website	Telephone	Percentage of mature students	Childcare
Havering College of Further and Higher Education	www.havering-college.ac.uk	01708 462801	n/a	✓
Hendon College	www.hendon.ac.uk	0208 200 8300	n/a	✓
Henley College Coventry	www.henley-cov.ac.uk	024 76 626300	n/a	✓
Herefordshire College of Art & Design	www.hereford-art-col.ac.uk	01432 273359	45	✓
Herefordshire College of Technology	www.hereford-tech.ac.uk	01432 365376	57	✓
Heriot-Watt University, Edinburgh	www.hw.ac.uk	0131 449 5111	15	✓
Hertford Regional College	www.hertreg.ac.uk	01992 411400	5	✓
Hertfordshire University	www.herts.ac.uk	01707 284800	20	✓
Heythrop College	www.heythrop.ac.uk	020 7795 6600	33	✗
Highbury College	www.highbury.ac.uk	02392 313281	n/a	✓
Hillcroft College	www.hillcroft.ac.uk	020 8399 2688	n/a	✗
Holborn College	www.holborncollege.ac.uk	020 7385 3377	n/a	✗
Huddersfield Technical College	www.huddcoll.ac.uk	01484 536521	n/a	✓
Huddersfield University	www.hud.ac.uk	01484 422288	16	✓
Hull University	www.hull.ac.uk	01482 466100	16	✓
Imperial College of Science, Technology and Medicine (University of London)	www.ic.ac.uk	020 7594 8014	1	✓
The Isle of Wight College	www.iwightc.ac.uk	01983 526631	n/a	✓
Keele University	www.keele.ac.uk	01782 584005	6	✓
Kent Institute of Art and Design	kiad.ac.uk	01622 757286	18	n/a

Institution	Website	Telephone	Percentage of mature students	Childcare
Kent University at Canterbury	www.ukc.ac.uk	01227 827272	14	✓
Kidderminster College	www.kidderminster.ac.uk	01562 820811	13	✓
King Alfred's Winchester	www.wkac.ac.uk	01962 841515	13	✓
King's College London	www.kcl.ac.uk	020 7836 5454	10	✓
Kingston University	www.kingston.ac.uk	0208 547 2000	18	✓
Lackham College	www.lackham.ac.uk	01249 466800	n/a	✗
Lampeter, University of Wales	www.lamp.ac.uk	01570 422351	33	✓
Lancaster & Morecambe College	www.lanmore.ac.uk	01524 66215	n/a	✓
Lancaster University	www.lancs.ac.uk	01524 65201	6	✓
Lansdowne College	www.lansdownecollege.com	020 7616 4400	0	✗
Leeds College of Art & Design	www.leeds-art.ac.uk	0113 202 8000	17	✗
Leeds College of Music	www.lcm.ac.uk	0113 222 3420	26	n/a
Leeds Metropolitan University	www.lmu.ac.uk	0113 283 2600	13	✓
Leeds: Park Lane College	www.parklanecoll.ac.uk	0113 216 2001	n/a	✓
Leeds, Trinity and All Saints College	www.tasc.ac.uk	0113 283 7123	7	✓
Leeds University	www.leeds.ac.uk	0113 233 3999	5	✓
Leicester College	www.lec.ac.uk	0116 224 2000	20	✓
Leicester University	www.le.ac.uk	0116 252 5281	9	✗
Leo Baeck College	www.lbc.ac.uk	020 8349 5600	100	✗
Lewisham College	www.lewisham.ac.uk	0208 692 0353	n/a	✓
Lincolnshire and Humberside University	www.ulh.ac.uk	01482 440550	25	✗

Institution	Website	Telephone	Percentage of mature students	Childcare
Liverpool Community College	www.liv-coll.ac.uk	0151 252 3000	37	✓
Liverpool Hope	www.hope.ac.uk	0151 291 3295	17	✓
The Liverpool Institute for Performing Arts	www.lipa.ac.uk	0151 330 3232	20	✗
Liverpool John Moores University	www.livjm.ac.uk	0151 231 5090	15	✓
Liverpool University	www.liv.ac.uk	0151 794 2000	8	✓
Llandrillo College, North Wales	www.llandrillo.ac.uk	01492 542338	44	✓
London Guildhall University	www.lgu.ac.uk	020 7320 1111	31	✓
The London Institute	www.linst.ac.uk	020 7514 6000	37	✓
London School of Economics and Political Science	www.lse.ac.uk	0207 955 7124/5	3	✓
London School of Jewish Studies		020 8203 6427	25	✗
Loughborough College	www.loucoll.ac.uk	01509 618375	n/a	✓
Loughborough University	www.lboro.ac.uk	01509 263171	4	✓
Lowestoft College	www.lowestoft.ac.uk	01502 583521	n/a	n/a
Luton University	www.luton.ac.uk	01582 489286	25	✓
Macclesfield College	www.macclesfield.ac.uk	01625 410000	n/a	✗
Manchester College of Arts and Technology	www.mancat.ac.uk	0161 953 5995	38	✗
Manchester Metropolitan University	www.mmu.ac.uk	0161 247 2000	14	✗
Manchester, UMIST	www.umist.ac.uk	0161 236 3311	7	✓
Manchester University	www.man.ac.uk	0161 275 2077	7	✓

Institution	Website	Telephone	Percentage of mature students	Childcare
Matthew Boulton College of Further and Higher Education	www.matthew-boulton.ac.uk	0121 446 4545	67	✓
Menai Coleg	www.menai.ac.uk	01248 370125	n/a	✗
Mid-Cheshire College	www.midchesh.ac.uk	01606 74444	0	✓
Middlesex University	www.mdx.ac.uk	020 8411 5898	25	✓
Napier University	www.napier.ac.uk	0500 353570	26	✗
Neath Port Talbot College	www.nptc.ac.uk	01639 648000	n/a	✓
Nescot	www.nescot.ac.uk	020 8394 3038	24	✓
Newcastle College	www.ncl-coll.ac.uk	0191 200 4000	18	✗
Newcastle upon Tyne University	www.ncl.ac.uk	0191 222 5594	7	✗
Newcastle-under-Lyme College	www.nulc.ac.uk	01782 715111	n/a	✗
New College Durham	www.newdur.ac.uk	0191 375 4210	22	✗
New College Nottingham	www.ncn.ac.uk	0115 9607201	n/a	✓
Newham College of Further Education	www.newhamcfe.ac.uk	020 8257 4000	36	✓
Newman College of Higher Education	www.newman.ac.uk	0121 476 1181	25	✗
Newport, University of Wales College	www.newport.ac.uk	01633 432432	33	n/a
North East Wales Institute of Higher Education	www.newi.ac.uk	01978 290666	20	✓
North East Worcestershire College	www.ne-worcs.ac.uk	01527 570020	20	✓
North Lincolnshire College	www.nlincs-coll.ac.uk	01522 876000	n/a	✓

Institution	Website	Telephone	Percentage of mature students	Childcare
North London University	www.unl.ac.uk	020 7753 3355	35	✓
North Tyneside College	www.ntyneside.ac.uk	0191 229 5000	44	✓
North Warwickshire and Hinckley College	www.nwarks-hinckley.ac.uk	02476 243000	17	✓
Northampton, University College	www.northampton.ac.uk	01604 735500	15	✗
Northbrook College Sussex	www.northbrook.ac.uk	01903 606060	27	✓
Northern College of Education	www.norcol.ac.uk	01224 283500	21	✗
Northumberland College	www.northland.ac.uk	01670 841200	0	✗
Northumbria University	www.unn.ac.uk	0191 2274777	18	✓
Norton Radstock College	www.nortcoll.ac.uk	01761 433161	n/a	✓
Norwich: City College	www.ccn.ac.uk	01603 773136	30	✓
Norwich School of Art and Design	www.nsad.ac.uk	01603 610561	22	✗
Nottingham Trent University	www.ntu.ac.uk	0115 941 8418	11	✓
Nottingham University	www.nottingham.ac.uk	0115 951 6565	5	✓
Oldham College	www.higher-education.co.uk	0800 269 480	n/a	✗
Oxford Brookes University	www.brookes.ac.uk	01865 483040	25	✓
Oxford College of Further Education	www.oxfe.ac.uk/ocfe	01865 245871	n/a	✓
Oxford University	www.ox.ac.uk	01865 270207	1	✓
Oxfordshire School of art and Design	www.northox.ac.uk	01295 252221	11	✓
Paisley University	www.paisley.ac.uk	0141 848 3727	38	✓
Pembrokeshire College	www.pembrokeshire.ac.uk	01437 765247	n/a	✓

Institution	Website	Telephone	Percentage of mature students	Childcare
The People's College Nottingham	www.peoples.ac.uk	0115 912 8582	n/a	✓
Pershore Group of Colleges	www.pershore.ac.uk	01386 552443	n/a	n/a
Peterborough Regional College	www.peterborough.ac.uk	01733 767366	n/a	n/a
Plymouth College of Art and Design	www.pcad.plym.ac.uk	01752 203434	26	✗
Plymouth University	www.plym.ac.uk	01752 232137	19	✓
Portsmouth University	www.port.ac.uk	02392 848484	13	✓
Queen Margaret University College, Edinburgh	www.qmuc.ac.uk	0131 317 3247	22	✓
Queen Mary and Westfield College (University of London)	www.qmw.ac.uk	020 7882 5555	11	✓
The Queen's University of Belfast	www.qub.ac.uk	028 9033 5081	6	✓
Ravensbourne College of Design and Communication	www.rave.ac.uk	0208 289 4900	32	n/a
Reading College and School of Arts & Design	www.reading-college.ac.uk	0800 371 434	37	✓
Reading University	www.rdg.ac.uk	0118 987 5123	9	✓
Regents Business School London	www.regents.ac.uk	020 7487 7654	0	✗
Ripon and York St John College	www.ucrysj.ac.uk	01904 656771	20	✓
Robert Gordon University	www.rgu.ac.uk	01224 262105	16	✓
Roehampton University	www.roehampton.ac.uk	020 8392 3232	12	✓
Rose Bruford College	www.bruford.ac.uk	020 8300 3024	16	✗

Institution	Website	Telephone	Percentage of mature students	Childcare
Rotherham College of Arts and Technology	www.rotherham.ac.uk	01709 362111	n/a	✓
Royal Agricultural College	www.royagcol.ac.uk	01285 889912	7	✗
Royal Holloway, University of London	www.rhul.ac.uk	01784 434455	8	✓
Royal Veterinary College	www.rvc.ac.uk	020 7468 5000	19	n/a
Ruskin College Oxford	www.ruskin.ac.uk	01865 310713	n/a	n/a
Rutland College Rycotewood College	www.rycote.ac.uk	01572 722863	n/a	✓
	www.rycote.ac.uk	01844 212501	58	✗
SAE Technology College	www.sae.edu	020 7609 2653	n/a	✗
Salford University	www.salford.ac.uk	0161 295 5000	22	✓
Salisbury College	www.salisbury.ac.uk	01722 344344	29	✓
Sandwell College	www.sandwell.ac.uk	0800 622006	31	✓
Scarborough University College	www.ucscarb.ac.uk	01723 362392	24	✗
School of Oriental & African Studies	www.soas.ac.uk	020 7637 2388	27	✗
School of Pharmacy	www.ulsop.ac.uk	020 7753 5831	21	✗
School of Slavonic and East European Studies	www.ssees.ac.uk	0171 862 8519	22	✓
Scottish Agricultural College	www.sac.ac.uk	01292 525350	27	✗
Sheffield College	www.sheffcol.ac.uk	0114 260 2216	19	✓
Sheffield Hallam University	www.shu.ac.uk	0114 2255555	15	✓
Sheffield University	www.sheffield.ac.uk	0114 222 2000	6	✓

Institution	Website	Telephone	Percentage of mature students	Childcare
Shrewsbury College of Arts and Technology	www.shrewsbury.ac.uk	01743 342342	26	✓
Solihull College	www.solihull.ac.uk	0121 678 7001	26	✓
Somerset College of Arts and Technology	www.somerset.ac.uk	01823 366366	25	✓
St George's Hospital Medical School	www.sghms.ac.uk	020 8725 5201	26	✓
St Helens College	www.sthelens.ac.uk	01744 733766	21	✓
St Loye's School of Health Studies	www.ex.ac.uk/affiliate/stloyes	01392 219774	49	✗
St Mark and St John's College	www.marjon.ac.uk	01752 636890	27	✓
St Martin's College, Lancaster	www.ucsm.ac.uk	01524 384444	25	✓
St Mary's College	www.smuc.ac.uk	020 8240 4029	10	✗
Soundwell College		0117 967 5101	n/a	✓
South Bank University	www.sbu.ac.uk	020 7815 7815	41	✓
South Birmingham College	www.sbirmc.ac.uk	0121 694 5002	n/a	✓
South Devon College		01803 406406	46	
South Downs College	www.southdowns.ac.uk	023 9279 7979	n/a	✓
South East Essex College	www.se-essex-college.ac.uk	01702 220400	n/a	✓
South Nottingham College	www.south-nottingham.ac.uk	0115 914 6400	n/a	✓
South Trafford College	www.stcoll.ac.uk	0161 952 4600	n/a	n/a
South Tyneside College	www.stc.ac.uk	0191 4273500	n/a	✗

Institution	Website	Telephone	Percentage of mature students	Childcare
Southampton City College	www.southampton-city.ac.uk	023 8048 4848	14	✓
Southampton Institute	www.solent.ac.uk	02380 319000	14	✗
Southampton University	www.soton.ac.uk	023 8059 5000	10	✓
Southport College	www.southport.mernet.org.uk	01704 500606	25	✗
Southwark College	www.southwark.ac.uk	020 7815 1526	30	✓
Staffordshire University	www.staffs.ac.uk	01782 294000	13	✓
Stamford College	www.stamford.ac.uk	01780 484300	n/a	✓
Stephenson College Coalville	www.stephensoncoll.ac.uk	01530 836136	n/a	✓
Stirling University	www.stir.ac.uk	01786 467044	13	✓
Stockport College of Further and Higher Education	www.stockport.ac.uk	0161 958 3100	34	✓
Stoke-on-Trent College	www.stokecoll.ac.uk	01782 208208	n/a	✓
Stranmillis University College	www.stran-ni.ac.uk	028 90 381271	6	✗
Stratford upon Avon College	www.strat-avon.ac.uk	01789 266245	n/a	n/a
Strathclyde University	www.strath.ac.uk	0141 552 4400	10	✓
Suffolk College	www.suffolk.ac.uk	01473 296369	32	✓
Sunderland University	www.sunderland.ac.uk	0191 515 3000	20	✓
Surrey Institute of Art and Design	www.surrart.ac.uk	01252 892609	19	✗
Surrey University	www.surrey.ac.uk	01483 300800	12	✓
Sussex University	www.sussex.ac.uk	01273 678416	15	✓
Sutton Coldfield College	www.sutcol.ac.uk	0121 355 5671	100	✓

Institution	Website	Telephone	Percentage of mature students	Childcare
Swansea College	www.swancoll.ac.uk	01792 284000	17	✓
Swansea Institute of Higher Education	www.sihe.ac.uk	01792 481000	20	✗
Swansea, University of Wales,	www.swan.ac.uk	01792 295111	12	✓
Swindon College	www.swindon-college.ac.uk	01793 498308	17	✓
Tameside College	www.tameside.ac.uk	0161 908 6789	0	✓
Teeside University	www.tees.ac.uk	01642 218121	25	✓
Thames Valley University	www.tvu.ac.uk	020 8579 5000	37	✗
Thomas Danby College	www.thomasdanby.ac.uk	0113 249 4912	n/a	✓
Tile Hill College of Further Education	www.tilehill.ac.uk	024 76694200	n/a	✓
Totton College	www.totton.ac.uk	02380 874 874	n/a	n/a
Trinity College Carmarthen		01267 676767	15	✓
Ulster University	www.ulst.ac.uk	02870 324221	11	✓
University College London	www.ucl.ac.uk	020 7679 3000	8	✓
Uxbridge College	www.uxbridge.ac.uk	01895 853333	n/a	✓
Wakefield College	www.wakcoll.ac.uk	01924 789111	n/a	✓
Wales University College of Medicine	www.uwcm.ac.uk	029 2074 2027	16	✓
Walsall College of Arts and Technology	www.walcat.ac.uk	01922 657000	n/a	✓
Warrington Collegiate Institute	www.warr.ac.uk	01925 494494	9	✓

Institution	Website	Telephone	Percentage of mature students	Childcare
Warwick University	www.csv.warwick.ac.uk	02476 523723	2	✓
Warwickshire College	www.warkscol.ac.uk	01926 318000	36	✓
Welsh College of Music and Drama	www.wcmd.ac.uk	029 2034 2854	10	✗
West Anglia College	www.col-westanglia.ac.uk	01553 761144	23	✓
West Cumbria College	www.wcc.ac.uk	01900 64331	20	✗
West Herts College, Watford	www.westherts.ac.uk	01923 812565	16	✓
West Nottinghamshire College	www.westnotts.ac.uk	01623 413626	n/a	n/a
West Thames College	www.west-thames.ac.uk	020 8326 2000	36	✓
Westhill College	www.westhill.ac.uk	0121 415 2206	29	✓
Westminster Kingsway College	www.westminster-cfe.ac.uk	020 7828 1222	39	✓
Westminster University	www.wmin.ac.uk	020 7911 5000	27	✓
Weston College	www.weston.ac.uk	01934 411411	75	✗
Weymouth College	www.weymouth.ac.uk	01305 208808	n/a	✓
Wigan and Leigh College		01942 761605	27	✓
Wigston College of Further Education	www.wigston-college.ac.uk	0116 288 5051	n/a	✓
Wimbledon School of Art	www.wimbledon.ac.uk	020 8408 5000	33	✗
Wirral Metropolitan College	www.wmc.ac.uk	0151 551 7777	51	✓
Wolverhampton University	www.wlv.ac.uk	01902 321000	24	✓
Worcester College of Technology	www.wortech.ac.uk	01905 725555	7	✓
Worcester University College	www.worc.ac.uk	01905 855111	25	✓
Writtle College	www.writtle.ac.uk	01245 424200	22	✗

Institution	Website	Telephone	Percentage of mature students	Childcare
Wye College	www.wye.ac.uk	01233 812401	11	✗
Yeovil College	www.yeovil-college.ac.uk	01935 845454	n/a	n/a
York College of Further and Higher Education	www.yorkcollege.ac.uk	01904 770200	30	✓
York University	www.york.ac.uk	01904 433533	5	✓
Yorkshire Coast College of Further and Higher Education	www.ycoastco.ac.uk	01723 372105	11	✓
Ystrad Mynach College	www.ystrad-mynach.ac.uk	01443 816888	n/a	✓

FURTHER INFORMATION

BOOKS AND OTHER RESOURCES

Bridging the Gap, published by DfEE (a booklet for disabled students).

The Careers Guide, published by Penguin.

The Directory of Grant-making Trusts, published by the Charities Aid Foundation.

Directory of Guidance Provision, published by DfEE.

Education Grants Directory, published by the Directory of Social Change.

Exams Without Anxiety, by David Acres, published by Deanhouse.

Financial Assistance for Students with Disabilities in Higher Education, published by Skill.

Financial Support for Higher Education Students: A Guide, published by DfEE (for people living in England and Wales).

Financial Support for Students: A Guide to Grants, Loans and Fees in Higher Education, published by Department of Education (for people living in Northern Ireland).

The Good Study Guide, by Andy Northedge, published by Open University Press.

The Grants Register, published by Macmillan.

Guide to Higher Education for People with Disabilities, published by UCAS and Skill.

Guide to Student's Allowances, published by the SAAS (for people living in Scotland).

Students' Money Matters, published by Trotman.

Students Support Sponsorship Funding Directory, published by CRAC/Hobsons.

UCAS Handbook, published by UCAS (details institutions, courses, and course codes).

University & College Entrance, published by UCAS (details entry requirements for all courses).

University Scholarships & Awards, published by Trotman.

Quotations in the text are from:

Access to Higher Education Course Directory 2001, published by Leeds Metropolitan University.

The Mature Student's Guide to Higher Education 2001, published by UCAS.

Arksey, H., Marchant, I. and Simmill, C. (eds) (1994) IHE Series – *Juggling for a Degree.*

Benn, R., Elliott, J. and Whaley, P. (eds) (1998) NIACE – *Educating Rita and Her Sisters.*

Coare, P. and Thomson, A. (eds) (1996) NIACE – *Through the Joy of Learning. Diary of 1,000 Adults.*

Tolmie, P. (ed.) (1998) IHE Series – *How I got my First Class Degree.*

Unattributed quotes are from the 1991 CNAA/UDACE counselling and guidance project for mature students, conducted by the authors.

USEFUL CONTACTS

Access courses database – available on the UCAS website.

Department for Education and Employment – Information line tel: 0800 731 9133. Website: www.dfee.gov.uk/studentsupport

Department of Social Security – Freeline Benefits Agency tel: 0800 666555. Website: www.dss.gov.uk

Edexcel Foundation – Tel: 0870 240 9800. Website: www.edexcel.org.uk

Educational Counselling and Credit Transfer Information Service (ECCTIS) – this database holds information on courses at UK universities and colleges of further and higher education –

Oriel House, Oriel Road, Cheltenham, Gloucestershire GL50 1XP. Tel: 01242 252627. Website: www.ecctis.co.uk

National Extension College – Michael Young Centre, Purbeck Road, Cambridge CB2 2HN. Tel: 01223 450200. Website: www.nec.ac.uk

The Open University Students Enquiry Service – PO Box 200, Milton Keynes MK7 6AA. Tel: 01908 653231. Website www.open.ac.uk

Skill – Chapter House, 18/20 Crucifix Lane, London SE1 3JW. Tel: 0800 3285050.

The Student Loans Company – 100 Bothwell Street, Glasgow G2 7JD. Tel: 0800 405010. Website: www.slc.co.uk

Trotman Publishing – 2 The Green, Richmond, Surrey TW9 1PL. Tel: 0208 486 1150. Website: www.trotman.co.uk/

UCAS – Rosehill, New Barn Lane, Cheltenham, Gloucestershire GL52 3LZ. Tel: 0242 227788. Website: www.ucas.com

Workers' Educational Association – Temple House, 17 Victoria Park Square, London E2 9PB Tel: 020 8983 1515.
Website: www.wea.org.uk

Student Awards Agency for Scotland – information on financial support for students living in Scotland – 3 Redheughs Rigg, South Gyle, Edinburgh EH12 9YT. Tel: 0131 556 8400.
Website: www.student-support-saas.gov.uk.

Department of Higher and Further Education Training and Employment – information on financial support for students living in Northern Ireland – Rathgael House, Balloo Road, Bangor, Co Down BT19 7PR. Tel: 02891 279279. Website: www.deni.gov.uk

For information about NHS bursaries in England – The NHS Student Grants Unit, Room 212C, Government Buildings, Norcross, Blackpool FY5 3TA. Tel: 01253 332627.

For information about NHS bursaries in Wales – Student Awards Unit, NHS Human Resources Division, National Assembly for Wales, Cathays Park, Cardiff CF10 3NQ. Tel: 029 20826893.

For information about NHS bursaries in Scotland – Student Awards Agency for Scotland, 3 Redheughs Rigg, South Gyle, Edinburgh EH12 9YT. Tel: 0131 244 4669.

For information about NHS bursaries in Northern Ireland –
The Department of Health, Social Services and Public Safety, Human Resources Directorate, Workforce Development Unit, Room 3B, Dundonald House, Upper Newtownards, Belfast BT4 3SF.

Educational Grants Advisory Service (EGAS) – provides independent advice on funding for further and higher education – 501–505 Kingsland Road, Dalston, London E8 4AU.
Tel: 020 7249 6636.

University of the Third Age – promotes lifelong learning among older people – 26 Harrison Street, London WC1H 8JG. Tel: 020 7837 8838
Website: www.u3a.org.uk

Association of Graduate Careers Advisory Services – centres throughout the country – Website: www.agcas.org.uk